Buy Your Home
SMARTER
with
Feng Shui

Ancient Secrets to Analyze and
Select Real Estate Wisely

Buy Your Home SMARTER with Feng Shui
Ancient Secrets to Analyze and Select Real Estate Wisely
By Holly Ziegler, M.A., Ed.

Published by **Dragon Chi Publications**™
P.O. Box 1036 • Arroyo Grande, CA 93421

Foreword by Denise Linn
Special supplement: Personal Directions and Flying Stars by Jami Lin
Edited by Arlene Winn, Karin Leonard, Kim Centeno, Rich Krietemeyer,
Prof. Melody DeMeritt, Elliot Jay Tanzer, and Geri Kelly.
Graphics by Jill Sterling
Original paper cuts from Yangchow, China
Photography by Holly Ziegler and
Anne Czajka (pages 59 and 162)

The purpose of this book is to educate and inform. The intent of the author
is to offer information of a general nature to assist the reader in purchasing
real estate. The author does not assume any responsibility for situations
people allege to have been produced by the interpretation or use of any of the
information contained in this book directly or indirectly.
Printed in the United States of America.

ISBN   0-9710652-0-9   (pbk.)

Library of Congress Control Number 2004092550

Also by Holly Ziegler…

Available at your favorite bookstore, and carried by the National Association of REALTORS® and the California Association of REALTORS®…

Sell Your Home FASTER with Feng Shui
Ancient Wisdom to Expedite the Sale of Real Estate
Dragon Chi Publications, 3rd printing, 2003

Feng Shui Your Workspace for Dummies
with Jennifer Lawler
Feng Shui Your Garden for Dummies
with Jennifer Lawler

Wiley Publishing, Inc. 2003

Buy Your Home
SMARTER
with
Feng Shui

Ancient Secrets to Analyze and
Select Real Estate Wisely

by

Holly Ziegler, M.A., Ed.

Dragon Chi Publications™
Arroyo Grande, California

Dedication

To my loving architect father
who taught me to pay close attention to the joy and
loveliness possible within every structure;

to Paige Genevieve as you begin your life path; and

to Anne Rice,
who opened my first beautiful
feng shui doors.

Acknowledgements

My special thanks to…

Denise Linn, my wondrous feng shui mentor,

Jill Sterling, my graphics specialist,

Jan Hayes, who always makes my way smooth, and

My faithful real estate ~ feng shui
clients and students who bring such sparkle to my life!

Chinese Proverb...

When there is light in the soul,
there is beauty in the person.

When there is beauty in the person,
there is harmony in the home.

When there is harmony in the home,
there is honor in the nation.

When there is honor in the nation,
there is peace in the world.

Table of Contents

Section I
Feng Shui Demystified

Section II
Feng Shui Secrets for Land and Homes

Tear-out Section

    Personal Priority List

    Property Check List

    List of Feng Shui Deal Breakers™

Foreword

by Denise Linn

Today I jumped in our truck and drove down the dusty, twisted country road that leads from our ranch into the nearby town which was founded by Spanish monks. I was on a mission to get a pastry bag for a dessert that my daughter was making. I remembered a specialty store that had opened the previous year that might have the item I wanted.

When I arrived, I saw a big sign in the window announcing, "Going Out of Business." I walked into the store. Everything was drastically marked down. When I asked why the store was going out of business, the owner looked distraught.

With grief in her voice, she said, "I don't understand it. We worked so hard here. When we bought this place we were sure we would have this shop for the rest of our lives. I don't know what went wrong."

I could feel how deeply distressed she was and I told her I was sorry she was going out of business. And silently, I sincerely wished that she had consulted with a feng shui expert or had read *Buy Your Home SMARTER with Feng Shui* before she and her husband had purchased the property. It might have saved the heartache they now faced.

As I looked at the location and the store, I could see so many things from a feng shui perspective that signaled potential difficulty for a business in that location. The front door (which is very important in feng shui) was not easily accessible. This limits access for chi (energy) and for customers to enter the store.

The previous business in the location had also struggled financially. (This is not usually a good sign in feng shui.) Additionally, when I entered the store, the layout made it very difficult to decide which way to go. This can be a metaphor for indecision. Customers may like what they see but may be undecided and not purchase anything.

Buying real estate can be one of the biggest decisions of your life. Whether you buy a home or a business location, it is immensely valuable to know what to look for — and what to avoid at all costs. Holly Ziegler's book can give you little known feng shui secrets that can help you make a wise choice when you are buying real estate. Holly's background as a successful REALTOR® and a respected feng shui teacher make this book a must for anyone buying real estate.

Denise Linn
Paso Robles, California

(Denise Linn is a feng shui master, international healer, writer, and lecturer. She has taught seminars in 19 countries and has written 14 books including the best-selling Sacred Space *and the award-winning* Sacred Legacies. *She has appeared on the Oprah Winfrey Show and in numerous documentaries, as well as on the Discovery, Lifetime Networks and BBC television.)*

Introduction

"The theory behind feng shui is that a life force flows through all things — buildings, hills, rivers, power lines, and people, and the manipulation of the force through the proper orientation of physical structures and placement of objects can enhance a person's wealth and good fortune. The first rule in real estate may one day read: Location, location... feng shui!"

— The New York Times

This book is for anyone getting ready to buy a home — and for real estate professionals who want to find the best house for their client. No doubt you are holding this book because you are a purchaser who wants to make the wisest decision possible. Whether this is your first home or your twenty-first, you have come to the right place.

Advantages of using feng shui savvy, as it applies to selecting your next real estate investment, are:

- ☯ You will feel better, luckier, and happier in a house with great feng shui.

- ☯ The property will be more energetically compatible with you — meeting your physical, emotional, and spiritual needs.

- ☯ The home will reflect your complete personality — what brings you happiness and, ultimately, fortunate blessings.

- ☯ It will be your sanctuary — a healing space away from the outside world.

☯ You will want to stay there a long time, not desiring to move unless some outside pressure forces you to relocate.

☯ Years from now, when you are the seller, you will smile on your way to the bank because your house will already have great feng shui — and will be so much easier to sell!

Buy Your Home SMARTER with Feng Shui is about progressive-thinking real estate — using ancient wisdom to find a home that not only feels wonderful, but also results in a great financial investment. It is a working manual for buyers and agents willing to think outside the box for better ways to accomplish a smart property purchase. You will receive clear and specific guidelines showing you what to look for in a property and what to be sure to avoid as you go house hunting.

I like to think of applying feng shui knowledge to selecting property as "higher consciousness real estate" — realizing that by using these techniques to choose from all the properties on the market, your choice will be made for reasons that make sense from a higher perspective. When you use feng shui wisdom to choose property, you will understand *why* you have made the choice you made and be more clear about the future implications of your investment that will serve you as you eventually become a seller.

Even if your purchase is for investment only and you do not intend to live in your new property, these feng shui guidelines will empower you as a buyer to look through new "feng shui eyes" as you preview each house to find the best value. *Buy Your Home SMARTER with Feng Shui* is not about teaching you feng shui in depth, but will introduce you to the feng shui principles that will help you choose a piece of real estate wisely.

This book is designed to be a working manual for the ordinary buyer or professional agent alike. At the end of most chapters you will find feng shui "smart moves" in the form of *Check Your Chi Lists* that give a (+) or (-) rating to over one hundred secrets relating to property selection. At the back of this book you will find a tear-out section with all these feng shui tips plus the *Feng Shui Property Appraisal*™ form that you will want to reference when you preview houses for sale. Also included in the tear-out section is a list of Feng Shui Deal Breakers™. I caution against purchasing properties with these feng shui conditions and you should proceed at your own risk — preferably, by getting back in your car and going on to the next house.

I suggest you make photocopies of this tear-out section and use them for each house you are serious about. Take them with you as you make your *Feng Shui Property Appraisal*™ explained in Chapter 6. These tools will empower you to analyze and finally purchase real estate with the highest and best feng shui information you will need to make a wise investment.

For over twelve years, I have used these techniques with hundreds of my clients, with varying budgets, in countless areas. They call and ask me to list their home for sale using feng shui guidelines to sell it quickly. Buyers want to purchase homes and land that have *good* feng shui, knowing their purchase will continually benefit them over time. Satisfied sellers refer their friends to me again and again.

As mentioned earlier, *this book is also designed for real estate professionals.* Many buyers already tell their real estate agents, "Show me only properties that have good feng shui!" Learning feng shui and applying its principles as you show and list property will put you far ahead of the professional learning curve and increase your sales. You will be the agent who wants the best for your clients and isn't shy about using knowledge considered a bit outside the box. Since feng shui works so well to sell homes and select property smarter, who cares!

To all buyers: it is your money and your choice. Applying feng shui principles in home selection may take more effort on your part; however, the quality of life you experience in your next house is worth it — *you* are worth it. Since purchasing a house will probably be the largest financial investment you make in your lifetime, it makes good sense to have all possible wisdom working for you. The essential manual for this purpose is now in your hands.

Choose wisely and enjoy the process!

Holly Ziegler,
Arroyo Grande, California

...from The Prophet

*And a merchant said, "Speak to us of Buying and Selling."
And he (Almustafa, the chosen and the beloved) answered
and said, "...It is in exchanging the gifts of the earth that
you shall find abundance and be satisfied. Yet unless the
exchange be in love and kindly justice, it will but lead some
to greed and others to hunger.*

*"When in the market place, you toilers of the sea and fields
and vineyards, meet the weavers and the potters and the
gatherers of spices, invoke then the master spirit of the earth,
to come into your midst and sanctify the scales and the
reckoning that weighs value against value.*

*"And suffer not the barren-handed to take part in your
transactions, who would sell their words for your labor. To
such men you should say, 'Come with us to the field, or go
with our brothers to the sea and cast your net; for the land
and the sea shall be bountiful even as to us'...*

*"...And before you leave the market place, see that no one
has gone his way with empty hands. For the master spirit
of the earth shall not sleep peacefully upon the wind till the
needs of the least of you are satisfied."*

— *Kahlil Gibran*

Section I

Feng Shui Demystified

Feng Shui 101 — The Basics

"The five essential factors that determine the quality of one's life:
first comes destiny, then comes luck… third is feng shui,
then right action, and education."

— Chinese Proverb

The Land of Ahhs!

Welcome to the world of feng shui (pronounced *fung schwaay*), what I like to call "the land of ahhs." As we drive along, houses with great feng shui get our attention and make us slow down. Without knowing exactly why, they bring joy to our hearts and smiles to our faces. When we are inside houses with good feng shui, we want to stay. Good feng shui affects us subtly, tapping into our feelings, making us respond with pure delight as we hear a small voice inside us exclaiming, "aah."

Feng shui is not a religion, nor is it superstition. Feng shui is a design philosophy about balance and harmony within environments. The principles of feng shui can be applied to residential, commercial, industrial properties, and vacant land. Often referred to as the "ancient art of placement," feng shui's principles are as effective in our modern world as they were in centuries past.

Feng shui is not about spending a lot of money and creating a mini-palace filled with designer appointments and fancy frills. Quite the contrary, with feng shui *less is best and the byword is "simplify."*

As feng shui Master Professor Wong expresses it, "…feng shui is probably the earliest form of environmental protectionism; it teaches that to destroy or pollute the earth is to destroy man's natural base. To improve one's self and to enjoy the environment is fundamental. The key element is selecting a site – the design of the house is secondary. A building should become a part of the site. Luxury does not necessarily equal good feng shui."[1]

In feng shui, the land is more important than the structure. Greater importance is placed on selecting a site than the building that will occupy the site. Ancient feng shui practitioners were always trained to work the land first, next the buildings, and lastly the rooms. Of course this feng shui philosophy supports what smart real estate investors already know — the most important aspect of choosing real estate is "location, location, location!"

Feng shui is an eco-science of harmony and balance that can enhance our homes and our lives. Feng shui is based on natural laws, the regular cycles of nature, and *how energy moves* through the universe. Feng shui is recognized today in most countries of the world; many cultures have similar guidelines that are for the most part basic common sense. By understanding how this energy flows throughout a space, including vacant land, feng shui principles teach sensitivity to how an environment feels, and how to maximize the harmony within that space.

The Chinese call energy "chi," and this word is what feng shui is all about: creating a positive flow of abundant, beneficial energy on your

---

[1] Feng shui intensive class taught by Master Prof. Wong in Beijing, China. Feng Shui Immersion Study Tour with Helen and James Jay, Oct. 2000.

land and within your house. It is important to realize that *all energy is interconnected*, so any change within a physical space, even a small one such as remodeling a single room of a house, will create energetic repercussions throughout the entire property. For now you can take the importance of chi, and the use of feng shui principles, on a leap of faith. However, after reading this book, you will be empowered with principles that have guided successful Asian real estate investors for centuries.

Be a Lucky "Looky Loo"

The serious study of feng shui is a life-long process that teaches us to enhance the harmony, balance, and good fortune in our lives. Feng shui's time-tested techniques can help you find a comfortable, energetically supportive, and ultimately auspicious dwelling for you and your family.

Just like gravity, you do not need to believe in feng shui for it to work and affect the world around you. Feng shui, both good and not so good, produces consequences whether we follow its guidelines or not. Similar to physics, when the apple falls from the tree, (gravity operates whether we understand it or not) feng shui will work its wonders on us, our land, homes, and office buildings.

Much more significant than a mere passing fad, feng shui is having a major impact on the world of real estate. *Sell Your Home FASTER with Feng Shui* and *Buy Your Home SMARTER with Feng Shui,* are carried at the highest professional level by the National Association of REALTORS®, the California Association of REALTORS®, and professional real estate associations across the country. It is fast becoming clear that buyers and sellers want feng shui information, and they expect their agents to provide it to them.

Just as fresh, pure air and water make us healthier and more energetic, so does good feng shui. This design science might be the original environmental impact study that recommended treading lightly on the earth, using natural products whenever possible, and avoiding that which does not energetically serve us. Using its suggestions to analyze and select real estate will give you an edge of special information that will amaze even the toughest skeptics.

Feng Shui Began in a Land Far, Far Away

Feng shui literally translates from the Chinese as "wind and water," representing the basic invisible and visible forces of nature that we cannot live without. Often referred to as the "art of placement" and the "environmental art/science of the twenty-first century," feng shui uses symbols and metaphors intertwined within its teachings. The importance of these metaphors, especially water as it relates to "abundance" will be explained in depth in later chapters.

Feng shui originally developed over three thousand years ago to aid in the selection of auspicious grave sites. It was referred to as "reading the land," and later, the art of "geomancy." Those who specialized in reading the land were called geomancers and were highly sought after, for it was they who could predict where crops would grow best, where rivers and creeks would carve their way in the spring torrents, and where the most favorable sites would be for graves of honored ancestors.

The Chinese believe in three forms of benevolent energy, or luck, based on the source from which the energy comes:

> ☯ *blessings from heaven* known as *"heaven luck,"*
>
> ☯ *right actions* and their consequences called *"man luck,"*

❧ *feng shui* or blessings from the land, called "*earth luck.*"

The more one cultivates "earth luck" the more blessings he or she will receive and the greater will be their prosperity and well-being. One of the fundamental "natal energies" (the inherent qualities similar to the energetic gene pool of a property such as location, direction, and energy flow) of feng shui is *where the structure sits.* Therefore, site selection is a primary focus of this book and is covered in depth in Chapters 7 and 8. *If you only read about one thing in this book, read about selecting a location!*

It Is Wise to Keep Our Ancestors Happy

Feng shui was originally known as *kan yu* and its practitioners were commissioned by the aristocracy to find the most favorable grave sites for revered ancestors. The theory was that if one's relatives were resting comfortably in a most auspicious location, they would shower their descendants with blessings and continue to protect and guide them in this life.

These feng shui specialists, later known as *hsien-sheng*, were taught to use their instinctive feelings to study the topography of the land. Feng shui scholars were also given the solemn responsibility of placing temples, and later imperial buildings, in such a way as to bring about the most abundant blessings of nature. The consequences of not following their advice were too terrible to think about. Rivers would wash temples away, strong winds would buffet the inhabitants, crops would not grow, and famine would ensue.

It Is Best Not to Disturb Mother Nature

Over the millennia, feng shui evolved into pure environmental common sense based on natural laws and the cycles of nature. Its guidelines taught people to carefully consider how to incorporate natural elements into buildings and how to place buildings so that the land is disturbed the least. Buildings, temples, and entire cities were laid out according to how the earth's energy flowed. Clues were based on mountains, hills, and land formations such as gullies and ravines. Careful attention was paid to topography such as forests, lakes, and rivers.

The best sites are where the winds are gentle, the waters run clear and pure, the landscape yields a sheltered and protected embrace, and the mountains (referred to as the back of the dragon), do not give rise to worries about disturbing that which is much better left alone. Feng shui became the original environmental awareness approach to building and designing structures. Buildings were laid out so that the back was to the harsh North winds. The entrances, whenever possible, faced the benevolent warmth and sunlight from the South.

The earth was tampered with only slightly. Tearing down forests, ripping apart hillsides, disturbing the soil deeply, or polluting soil and rivers, would only invite natural disasters unleashing bad feng shui. The wise builder would never tempt the fates this way.

The Feng Shui of Wind and Water

Because water will eventually have its own way, we must be educated in the habits of water, or pay the penalty. Man can build dams and bridges, and can place buildings on stilts, but eventually water will assert itself and the hundred-year flood will come, taking all in its path. Of course, the temples and cities built above the high watermark will survive and their planners inwardly smile at their own wisdom of fortunate placement, saying prayers for those who did not heed the clues to water's greatest ravages.

Serious students of feng shui were also studying how Mother Nature hurled her winds and storms at a site. Having a beautiful temple or a grand imperial building with an awesome view is great, but if you can't step outside and enjoy the beauty of a tranquil breeze, something is wrong. Winds, and the direction from which they come, are of particular interest in selecting a site for a single building or an entire city. To put oneself directly in the path of a windstorm is not using feng shui wisdom.

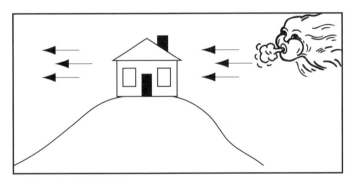

House at top of hill receives full impact of wind (shui) energy.

Finally, Feng Shui Came to the People

As feng shui developed and was put to expanded use by wealthy and educated people, its concepts began to filter down to the common man. When it became obvious that feng shui produced such beneficial results, families of the less affluent classes quickly learned to make use of it to improve their own positions in life.

Soon an entire society was incorporating the guidelines of this natural design science. It was becoming clear that by following feng shui principles, cities flourished, crops grew abundantly, and people found more harmony and overall well-being in their lives. That is why this ancient art of placement has survived so well to the present day. It works!

Shanghai, Beijing, and Singapore are examples of major cities designed in accordance with feng shui; all of them were laid out to have the protection of the Four Celestial Animals in the form of the *black tortoise* (mountains) to the rear, the bounty and majesty of the *crimson phoenix* (sea) in the foreground, and the auspicious guardians of the sleeping *green dragon* and the *white tiger* (sloping hillsides) gently to the east and the west. This configuration is often referred to as the classic "armchair" position, and is presented in depth in Chapters 3 and 8.

Classic (Armchair) Position for Site Placement

Feng Shui Armchair Location

Today, feng shui is practiced on a world-wide scale beyond the early feng shui practitioners' wildest dreams. The city of Hong Kong is the perfect example of feng shui principles on a large scale. When visiting this thriving metropolis, one can even sign up for a "Feng Shui Tour" of the city!

Different Schools Use Different Rules

Arlene and Ira are looking for a birthday gift for their friend Marion. Marion and her husband Paul are thinking about moving. Marion had told Arlene about an intriguing show she had seen on PBS that showed how a design philosophy called "feng shui" revealed specific guidelines for choosing properties. Arlene decided a perfect gift for her friend would be a feng shui book.

In the bookstore, Arlene found nearly a hundred titles to choose from on feng shui. She groaned because she did not have all day to spend on this project — so she began leafing through what looked like books for beginners.

Arlene quickly realized this might not be so easy. Some books had drawings of a compass with South at the top and North at the bottom. Marion would probably not go for that. Other volumes were beautiful coffee table books with many pictures, but not much explanation. Marion needed as much guidance as possible.

Finally, Arlene found several books that talked about shapes of lots, floor plans of homes, and specifics on what to avoid in order for the house and property to have the best feng shui. The books had many examples and photographs with clear explanations. Yes! Useful information plus enjoyable reading. The very thing!

As with any discipline, feng shui has various viewpoints and schools of thought. Authors of different books about feng shui base their information on the "school" of feng shui they follow. This practice can be a bit confusing for the feng shui novice. However, the brief descriptions that follow will give you some basic information about the different approaches common to each school and will help guide you as you search for books to help you beyond this text.

Form School

Approximately three thousand years ago, the Form School was feng shui's original approach to analyzing the land. It began in the south of China where extreme mountain formations dominated the landscape. Form school feng shui gave instruction on placement of the ideal sites for graves, agricultural planting, and placement of temples and dwellings on clues from land formations, water-courses, mountains, and valleys as they would interact together, giving the most auspicious and practical building locations.

Form School feng shui is widely used today, even by other schools because its information about "reading" the land is so pertinent, whether for a residential or commercial site. Without this fundamental Form School assessment of the energy of the land, the rest of the interpretation of feng shui would be based on incomplete data.

Realizing they need feng shui information, real estate developers are now calling in feng shui consultants to help position entire subdivisions. Speculators who want to build golf courses, athletic complexes, and shopping malls are employing feng shui masters to assist these sophisticated investors in site placement and other critical design information. They want all the cards of good fortune in their hands.

Compass School

Approximately 2,000 years ago in the North of China, early feng shui practitioners developed a unique compass called a *"luo pan"* which measured the *"sitting" and "facing"* directions of structures. The luo pan is a handheld device with a floating circular plate with as many as 38 concentric rings and a magnetic compass in the center. The luo pan enabled practitioners to predict the prevailing auspicious or adverse energetic influences and their likely effects on any temple or dwelling.

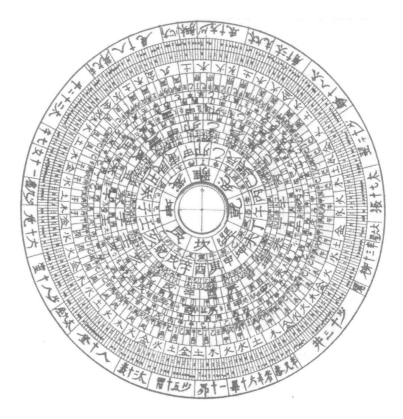

Early Feng Shui Luo Pan Compass

The luo pan was the primary tool of Compass School practitioners. It is still used to identify specific directions of a dwelling and thus determine the most auspicious energy of a structure based on when the roof was put on the house (and the energy was sealed in) or when the occupants moved into the house.

When giving a professional consultation for a home or business, an experienced feng shui consultant will take a careful reading using this special compass and thus be able to identify the Best Directions and Flying Star energies (the astrological time-based aspect of feng shui) associated with the house and its occupants.

Traditional feng shui, often referred to as Compass School, is based primarily on the *direction* a house faces. The direction is determined by the placement of the front door (called the "mouth of chi") as well as the front of a building as it faces the street or primary source of outside energy. Accurate compass readings from the front door (as one faces out) become quite important as these compass readings form the groundwork for all other determinations.

Using detailed and specific mathematical calculations, Compass School practitioners are adept at reading the unique Chinese luo-pan compass which takes a great amount of study and practice. This feng shui compass is said to predate the mariner's compass and its modern version is used today by Compass School practitioners world wide.

Techniques for reading a basic compass and determining the facing direction of a structure are explained in Chapter 6 and in the Special Supplement. The elemental natal energy of various locations within the house and how they can be amplified or mitigated can then be calculated to encourage the most beneficial chi for a dwelling and its inhabitants.

Another classical form of Compass School feng shui, known as *Flying*

Star feng shui, deals not only with the direction the house faces and sits, but also with *time*. Flying Star feng shui considers the astrological application and bases its calculations on *when* the house was built, *when* the mistress and master of the dwelling were born, and *when* they moved into the house. Even today, feng shui masters sometimes differ on which date to use. Compass School and its related forms of feng shui are practiced world-wide and are especially popular in Europe and the Far East.

Black Tibetan Sect (or Black Hat) School

Brought to the West from China by H.H. Professor Thomas Lin Yun approximately 40 years ago, Black Hat's School of feng shui has its roots in Buddhist and Taoist traditions. Its basis for reading the energy of a building or commercial site depends upon the *location* (not the direction) of the "mouth of chi," the feng shui term for the primary door of a structure.

Black Sect uses a more transcendental approach to feng shui and also considers the setting of "intention" as fundamental to achieving maximum results from remedies for feng shui problems. Coming more from an art than a scientific method, followers of Black Sect often utilize mirrors, wind chimes, and crystals to enhance the flow of chi within a space.

An ancient octagonal energy template called the *bagua*, is the basis for determining the locations of the Eight Life Aspirations, (explained in the next chapter). The Black Sect School of feng shui is very popular in the United States and has a global following.

Intuitive Feng Shui

In addition to the primary schools of feng shui, you may hear references to "intuitive feng shui." Intuitive feng shui is simply what most artists and designers practice when they have no formal training in any particular school of feng shui, and is that innate sense of beauty and design that some people are born with.

Intuitive feng shui is not a true school, however, and is more like an inherent talent or skill. Similar to a "sixth sense," many people possess this gift of knowing how to harmoniously place things and decorate with a feeling for balance that delights the senses and feeds the spirit.

The Feng Shui Bottom Line

Many highly respected practitioners use a variety of approaches to achieve the ultimate goal of feng shui: harmony, overall well-being, fortunate blessings, and balance within one's space and personal world. No matter which school you are most comfortable with, after applying feng shui guidelines, your home or office will have more freely moving energy, and feel more tranquil and comfortable.

In my own feng shui practice, I always incorporate the Form School, calculate the owners' Personal Directions, and work with Compass School energy. I find the bagua overlaid on a floor plan is helpful to clients, and I empower the central tai chi area of a structure whenever possible. I am a firm believer in setting powerful intentions along with incorporating the Five Elements for feng shui solutions. The positive results are very effective and usually speedy. These techniques keep clients coming back for more consultations, and they constantly refer me to their friends and family.

Think of using feng shui principles to analyze and buy property as a new game you are learning to play. There are a few basic rules and guidelines, along with a great deal of personal interpretation, of how a site makes you feel, and you can count on plenty of fun along the way. It is an extremely creative and enjoyable process. The home you select will energetically support you and be more enjoyable; your friends will comment on how great it feels to be there. The most important thing to remember is that you are playing this game for yourself, and the bottom line is — you will be the winner!

For Best Results, Use your Intuition

As you continue to learn the feng shui secrets that will assist you with selecting your new home, you will want to constantly be in touch with your inner feelings (intuition) about property. Just as your sense of balance helps you to walk, your intuition will help guide you to choose real estate wisely. I urge you to frequently "check in" with that special part of yourself that quietly whispers, "I really like it here" or, "This house is okay, but there is something that does not feel quite right."

Together with the many practical feng shui tips you will learn in this book, remember that feng shui is about your *feelings* for a property (as you approach the site, walk the grounds, go up the front path, stand on the front porch, open the door, step inside, and go through the various rooms). As you practice tapping into your feelings, this skill becomes easier.

You need to ask yourself while you are in the house, "How do I *feel* here?" Be very honest as you go through this process; stop and ask yourself: Are there any areas where you felt uneasy, uncomfortable, unprotected, or energetically puzzled in any way? This habit of

16

consciously asking how you feel takes time to develop and requires constant practice. After doing this with three or four homes, you will develop confidence and your perceptions will become increasingly clear and defined.

What You Perceive *Is* Your Reality

Your perceptions make sense to you on both an inner and an outer level. You may *like* a house because it looks great from the outside and is close to work — and you may have good *feelings* about a house because it is filled with natural sunlight, has a lovely view, and you enjoy being there.

Particularly sensitive people are able to detect negative energy as soon as they walk through the door of a house. If you are having persistent feelings of anxiety about a house or you are not able to relax, save your time and energy and go on to the next property. Do not allow yourself to be talked into a place where you are uneasy even if someone else has good reasons; this is a big feng shui mistake.

What your senses are responding to is negative or stuck energy in some form. You may be picking up these negative energy from a source that is not readily apparent (such as precursor energy that will be explained in Chapter 10). Whatever the source, if you allow other considerations to overcome your instincts, you will regret the purchase of a particular house because the negative feelings will slowly wear you down.

The Murmurings of a Higher Voice

I wish real estate agents would ask their clients, "How does this property make you *feel*?" Your agent might ask, "How do you *like* this house?" But that question misses the feng shui point. There is a distinction between feelings — and likes and dislikes. Feelings have to do with your inner comfort zone and defy being weighed or measured. You cannot order a pint of "relaxed" or "comfortable" (feelings) the way you order a pint of Ben and Jerry's ice cream (likes). You may *like* ice cream and not *feel* good about it after getting on the scale!

I like to think of intuitive feelings as the voice from our higher selves that whispers to us what is for our highest and best good. The "good" referred to here is not necessarily money in the bank or the new promotion, as much as it is information for our greater long-term happiness and our energetic and spiritual growth.

Usually when we follow our passion (our intuition) a desired promotion or the money will come because we are acting from a deeper source. Our higher self always knows what is best for us. If we do not pay attention to this "inner advice" it does not mean the information is not in our best interest; we have unfortunately chosen to ignore it.

So too with assessing real estate. Feelings have to do with our subtle anatomy, our inner hallowed place where we respond to external stimuli, be it a house, a book we read, a program we watch, or a person with whom we fall in love. Likes and dislikes are superficially similar, but are not the same. The sooner you trust that deeper knowing of your intuition, the sooner you will make quantum leaps toward applying your version of "intuitive" feng shui.

Buyers Have Different Feng Shui Needs from Sellers

In my first book, *Sell Your Home FASTER with Feng Shui*, I was concerned with the owners of properties and how to help them sell their homes quickly using feng shui principles. I focused on helping them energetically "release" the house to make way for the new buyer. However, the goal of most purchasers is to stay in their next house for a long time, or at least savor to the fullest whatever time they do live there; they are not letting go, they are moving in!

Buyers need to have the greatest amount of feng shui information on their side in order to make a smart decision about which house to purchase. The ideal feng shui house will not merely provide a roof over their heads, but will serve the homeowners' highest energetic needs, bringing harmony, balance, good fortune, and overall well-being into their lives.

To give you the greatest quality of feng shui information, this book refers to "Personal Directions" frequently. A Special Supplement devoted to this subject by my dear friend and internationally recognized feng shui author, Jami Lin, is included at the back of this book. Jami also includes information about a detailed form of feng shui referred to as "Flying Stars." As mentioned earlier, the Flying Stars approach deals with feng shui *in time* and contains a more astrological theory about bringing balance, harmony and good luck into one's life based on when new occupants move into the house. (Some masters base this data on when the house was constructed.)

Flying Star data is for those readers who want a very personalized form of feng shui assistance in purchasing a home. Some buyers may not feel the need to pursue this. *It is included for whomever feels it will serve their highest needs.* If it is not your cup of tea, that is fine and I advise you not to be concerned with it. There is more than enough other feng shui information to keep you fully occupied! Any time you feel you need advanced assistance, I encourage you to call in a qualified feng shui consultant to help in your selection of a new home. An excellent source for trained consultants for most geographic areas in the United States is: **www.fengshuidirectory.com**.

Understanding Chi
and the Bagua

Isadora and Alan have decided enough is enough and something has to be done — quickly! After not seeing them for three years, Alan's mother is coming to visit next week and the guest room is filled with their travel gear, camping equipment, boxes of slides from trips, and hiking paraphernalia. When Alan and Isadora first moved in, some of this stuff might have fit in the garage, but now that too is full of boxes, tools, and automotive equipment.

Neither Isadora nor Alan has been feeling too great lately and little things are starting to get on their nerves. Even looking through those two big piles of travel magazines in the corner of the dining room is not fun anymore. Something is wrong. Intuitively, Isadora blames her depression and Alan's confusion on all their stuff — they are choking on clutter.

Unless they put mother in bed with them, the guest room has got to be cleaned out now! Reluctant to spend money on a storage unit, Alan devises a plan of attack. With boxes from the local grocery store, he and Isadora begin to sort through the guest room confusion.

Since they have not been hiking in several years, and have been saving the equipment and camping gear for some sunny day, they decide to send it all to the local Goodwill. After organizing the slides, they will enjoy looking at them one last time with Mom.

Grinning as they work, Alan and Isadora dig in, determined not to stop until the job is done. Later, looking at their orderly, reclaimed guest room, they celebrate by treating themselves to a well deserved dinner at their favorite restaurant. They are feeling better already.

Einstein Would Have Loved Feng Shui

If you enjoy studying natural science and various forms of energy, you will love feng shui, because energy is what this ancient art of environmental design is all about. *Chi*, as mentioned earlier, is the Chinese word for energy. It translates as life breath, universal energy, the all-encompassing life force that permeates the universe, the earth, and all living things, including you and me.

You do not have to be an Einstein to appreciate the forces of energy and most cultures have a word for this concept of chi: in Japanese it is *ki*, in India it is *prana*, for the ancient Romans, *spiritus*, *pneuma* in Greek, *ruah* in Hebrew, and *rhor* in Arabic. Feng shui is predicated on the movement of chi; to understand feng shui, you need to understand this chi energy — what it is, how it operates within a space, and its effect on the environment and on ourselves.

The All-Encompassing River of Chi

Chi energy is everywhere and fills *all* spaces — our bodies, our dwellings, our offices, auditoriums, football stadiums, forests, oceans, and the atmosphere. It is easy to understand chi if you think of a flowing river filling every corner, rivulet, and eddy all the way to the banks.

When moving in a *straight line*, the river is restless and flows quickly, sometimes destructively. Its speed and power can erode the banks, taking out piers and pilings. This fast flowing river of chi needs to be slowed down in order to bring tranquility and harmony to a space.

However, when the river of chi *meanders*, the water moves more slowly and gently. The energy of the water does not cause destruction. The area feels more tranquil, inviting, and peaceful — there is a sense of a beautiful comfort zone working its magic.

A serene environment makes us want to
relax and stay awhile.

Upon finding such a serene environment, most of us would want to spread out a blanket on the bank of this river and stay awhile. Our inner tranquility barometer is at a high point and we feel like resting... we feel at home.

The old phrase "Home, Sweet Home" has such special meaning for most of us. The adjective "sweet" has a subtle, yet powerful impact. This sweet spot is what we want to find in the new house we purchase — a place where our energy will feel like staying and resting. Large or small, simple or grand — this is our castle, our sacred space.

Applying this concept of freely moving chi to homes, one of the things to look for is a floor plan where the energy of the dwelling (interior chi), moves easily and gently through the space. Tiny rooms, lots of interior angles, irregular shaped spaces, make for a difficult flow of positive chi.

Stuck Chi — Release It and Simplify

Imagine a clear and sparkling stream of water moving through a gentle brook — where the chi is moving ideally. However, if off to one side, the water becomes trapped in an eddy, the movement stops, the water cannot flow easily; it eventually becomes murky and stagnant — in feng shui speak, this chi is "stuck."

Stuck chi is like stagnant water…
it goes nowhere and brings negative energy to an environment.

To maintain a positive movement of energy we try to avoid areas of stuck chi whenever possible. Just as Isadora and Alan experienced in their guest room with piles of newspapers or magazines on the floor, dirty laundry in corners, tables groaning with stacks of papers, garages stacked with boxes, overloaded kitchen counter-tops — all this clutter is stuck chi!

This "stuff" energetically weighs us down, blocks our progress, adds confusion to our lives, and adds to our inability to move forward in our daily activities. We hit an energetic wall where we are stuck trying to decide if we are Tweedle Dee or Tweedle Dum.

All that extra stuff is the worst enemy of good feng shui and requires constant vigilance to keep our environment uncluttered so this magic of easy-flowing chi can work. Most of us are prone to collecting and hoarding the small and useless things we think we will need one day, thinking that someday it will all come in handy. "Someday" is not in our palm pilots or our day planners — and that rare emergency seldom arrives. We do not realize the time and energy it takes to climb over the stored clutter, wade through it, and pack it all up. When the garage will not hold any more, we rent storage units — this is a serious illness. Feng shui to the rescue!

The Toll of Clutter

As Thoreau is reported to have said to Emerson, "Simplify, simplify, simplify!" Emerson then replied, "Henry, one 'simplify' would have been enough!" Most of us want to simplify, pare down, and make do with less. That is why we feel so wonderful when we manage to clean out a drawer, a closet, or a garage. It is pure joy to unclutter our lives.

Typical garage, filled with everything but a car.

Better than Green Tea or Vitamin B$_{12}$

This stuck chi needs to be cleared and released or it will be a constant source of confusion and disharmony (otherwise known as dis-ease). Stuck chi on a personal level manifests as depression; we feel sluggish and unable to easily move forward with our daily tasks. A sense of lethargy takes over and sometimes even simple jobs seem huge. In other words, we cannot handle it all so we escape to the land of the couch potato.

Most of us need some semblance of order in our lives to make progress. When our desks get cluttered we find it difficult to get our work done; when our homes become cluttered our outlook and state of mind are negatively affected. Because *our homes are a direct reflection of ourselves*, a cluttered house can be an indicator of a cluttered mind — confused, bewildered, and in a major rut.

Just like taking an organic tonic or elixir that gives our bodies an energetic lift, the faster we banish clutter the sooner we will feel lighter, freer, happier, and more focused. Try clearing away some of your own stuck chi and see how much lighter and more focused you feel. I guarantee that as soon as you take positive action to eliminate your clutter you will feel as though you have been given a "charge" of new strength and positive energy. You will feel better than if you have had a large dose of green tea or vitamin B_{12}!

Rivers of Old Are the Streets of Today

Another form of chi is "fast-moving" chi, usually in the form of straight lines such as busy streets and highways. In ancient times, rivers and dirt pathways were the byways for people moving from one place to another. In today's world, freeways, interstate highways, major boulevards, and ordinary streets are the byways of our transportation system.

Obviously some roads are busier and have more heavy traffic energy than others. In feng shui, these roads, especially very busy streets in residential districts, are the equivalent of a well-used and fast-flowing river. To live on an exceptionally busy street is to invite the stressful, frantic chi of automobiles, trucks, headlights, etc. in to your sacred space.

If you fall in love with a house on a busy street, you will want to examine your decision carefully. The street will only get busier — and your need for peace and quiet will grow exponentially. Do not fool yourself by thinking you will "get used to the traffic." You will get used to it over time, like getting used to having a root canal, and you will wish you had put your money down in a more quiet location.

Avoid "Poison Arrows," Alias *Sha* Chi

This fast-moving chi is known as "*sha chi*" — literally translated as "noxious vapor" or "killing breath." This energetic poison arrow is not good feng shui and should be avoided wherever possible. In addition to busy streets, another example of sha chi is extremely pointy objects, such as exaggerated roof lines that appear to be "aimed" at another (your potential) property. We can see other forms of this negative energy in countless ways in our environment that send cutting chi our way. Often sha chi will show up as massive or strong electrical elements: high power lines, large satellite dishes, radio antennae, and microwave stations.

Sha chi is like an energetic finger constantly pointing at you, causing uneasiness, discomfort, and subtle agitation. This is an inner level of distress; one does not feel tranquil or at ease with constant sha chi aimed in our direction. Water towers and massive water storage tanks also harbor sha chi. Their overpowering size is like a huge wave of water waiting to wash over you.

Sha chi can also emanate from within a dwelling, such as from a dominant inner corner that protrudes into a room. A simple way to correct this condition is to cover the guilty corner in any way that appeals to you. Some examples of good ways to neutralize sha chi from an inner corner are to hang or place a plant at the corner, or to hang a decorative piece of fabric or wall-hanging over it. You do not want a pointy corner from a wall or pointy piece of furniture sending you cutting energy while you sleep, work at your desk, or cook in the kitchen.

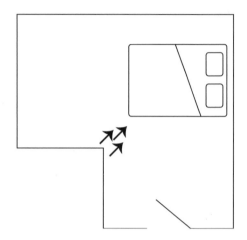

Sharp inner corner sends sha chi within a room.

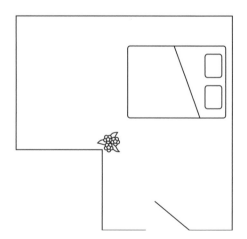

Placing a plant or hanging a decorative fabric over the sharp inner corner will mitigate the sha energy.

Exaggerated pointy roofline emanates sha chi.

Massive Sha Energy of Water Storage Tank

Following, you will see other examples of sha chi in various forms. As you begin to look at your prospective neighborhood with your newly acquired feng shui eyes, you will begin to notice many examples that should be avoided if you are to find a property with good feng shui. Remember that *location is everything — more important than the house itself.* A fancy decorating plan cannot correct a poor choice in site selection, especially a location fraught with powerful sha chi that you are unable to correct.

Sha Energy from Typical Transformer

Microwave Booster Station

Sha Energy from Electric Power Station

High Power Lines Found in Many Neighborhoods

Not only are these various forms of electric transmitters sources of dangerous electromagnetic energy, they are visually ugly and are definite sha poison arrows. Avoid this kind of sha chi in your neighborhood when selecting your new property. More will be discussed about sha chi when site selection is covered in Chapters 7 and 8. For now it is important to be aware that it exists. Remedies for sha chi are found in Appendix C.

The Emperor and the Tortoise

Legend has it that feng shui originated about 2900 B.C. with the Emperor Fu Hsi, who some consider to be the father of Chinese civilization. As the story goes, while he sat meditating on the banks of the Lo River, a giant tortoise emerged from the water and came to rest nearby.

Profoundly inspired, Fu Hsi saw the shell's orderly lined markings, which turned out to be the pattern for the numbers found within the *lo-shu* or *Magic Square* which became fundamental to feng shui. This marking sequence was further developed by the Duke of Chou into the trigrams of the *I Ching,* or *The Book of Changes.* These trigrams, which he later doubled, are referred to as hexagrams. These intricate and often complicated aspects of feng shui are not explored in this book; you don't need to know these things to analyze and select real estate. However, if you want more information about trigrams, hexagrams, or the Magic Square. I would recommend Steven Skinner's excellent text, *Flying Star Feng Shui.*

The mathematical construct of the Magic Square is uniquely arranged so that all the numbers from one through nine add up to "fifteen" in any direction. This Magic Square became the foundation for feng shui, Chinese numerology and astrology, and the construct of the Nine Star Ki. [1]

4	9	2
3	5	7
8	1	6

The Lo-Shu Numbers of the Magic Square

---

[1] *Feng Shui for Beginners,* Richard Webster, p. 77.
[2] Ibid, p. 11.

Ancient Wisdom of the *I Ching*

This ancient art of placement and spatial harmony that is feng shui is based on the evolving teachings from the *I Ching*, or *Book of Changes*. This oldest book known in China is in turn based on the Taoist application of the opposing forces of yin and yang which we will discuss in depth in the next chapter.

The *I Ching* is said to be the only Confucian text to survive the great *Burning of Books* in 215 B.C. It is believed to contain the secrets of life and has had an incalculable effect on Chinese culture and philosophy.[2] The *I Ching* is still widely read and consulted by philosophers and students of Eastern thought. Its wisdom applies as much today as it did ages ago.

Written to assist people in understanding and coping with the challenges of change, the *I Ching* is a guide to right conduct, giving instruction about how to lead a successful and fulfilling life from birth until death. The *I Ching* describes the universe as a constantly moving and changing entity and reveals how the superior man (and woman) would behave under difficult circumstances. In approximately 1200 B.C., King Wen, the Duke of Chou, and later Confucius, expanded the earlier version of the *I Ching*. The book evolved, becoming a written body of knowledge that further codified the practice of feng shui by giving it a formal structure.

From the 17th to the 20th centuries, Confucianism and Taoism had enormous influence on Chinese government and public life, reflected in a respect for both nature's beauty and a strict social order. Education was highly prized, but only serious scholars could rise to an elevated status within the imperial court, which had extremely rigid and formal criteria.

Confucius

During this same period, an emphasis on the more delicate arts of painting, poetry, and calligraphy were required for the truly educated person. Chinese architecture came into its own, and perfection in landscaping became a highly specialized and prized skill. Over the centuries, this feng shui art of placement grew from a series of guidelines dealing with resting-places for the dead into an active philosophy of designing homes for the living.

The lo shu grid forms the basis for the trigrams of the *I Ching* and the feng shui bagua, which are explained in the following section. The Magic Square is also fundamental to Chinese astrology and Flying Star feng shui discussed in the Special Supplement immediately following Chapter 10.

The Powerful Feng Shui Bagua

The octagonal shaped "energy template" of feng shui called the *bagua* originated early in Chinese history. Derived directly from the lo-shu grid, the bagua is designed to organize and provide a placement guide for the *Eight Life Aspirations* explained further in this chapter plus the central *tai chi*, or energetic hub (making a total of nine areas of energy). Grasping the concept of the bagua is important to understanding feng shui and it is continually referred to in various readings and applications to land and structures. Black Sect School makes extensive use of the bagua in its implementations of feng shui guidelines.

The bagua is explained briefly here because throughout this book I refer to various aspects of the bagua as they apply to selecting real estate. However, only the briefest information about the bagua is included in this book to help you to analyze what is on the market and to choose property wisely. (A thorough analysis and explanation of the intricacies of the ancient bagua would fill an entire book.) The bagua is made up of the eight aspects of life to which the Chinese gave the greatest importance. It is important to know that *each of these areas of our life influences all the others;* if any one of these Life Aspirations (sometimes referred to as "kuas") is seriously out of balance, it will negatively affect the others and subsequently the harmony in one's life and family will be jeopardized.

Feng shui is all about achieving harmony and balance — balance in our relationships, work, spirit, family, material well-being, friends, and society. Since *our home is a direct reflection of ourselves*, it follows that achieving harmony and balance both inside and outside our castle is fundamental.

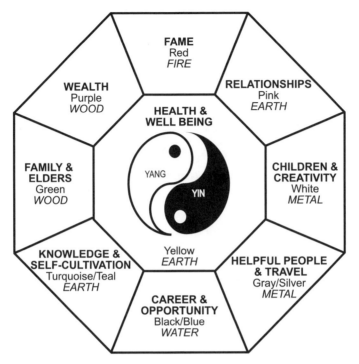

The Traditional Bagua Showing Eight Life Aspirations

Associated Colors and Elements

The eight kuas or Life Aspirations of the bagua, with their associated Direction, Element, and shape are:

Career – the way in which we look at our personal world and the satisfaction (or lack of it) that we find in our daily work (North, Water Element, amorphous or fluid shape, the colors deep blue and black)

Knowledge and Self Cultivation – our introspective self as we seek greater wisdom in our mind and heart – the area where we prepare intellectually for a new area of study, and develop kindness and compassion (Northeast, Earth Element, shape of the square, the colors teal blue, and yellow)

__Elders and Health__ – the way we relate to our biological family, parents and forebears, and the love, respect, and healing that goes along with these relationships; physical health (East, Wood Element, shape of a column or a tree trunk, the color green)

__Wealth and Abundance__ – not just money in the bank, but also the abundance that fills our heart; having enough for our needs and sufficiency to share with others (Southeast, Wood Element, shape of a column or smaller trees, the colors green and purple)

__Fame and Reputation__ – how the world looks at us, our personal integrity and social honor among our peers (South, Fire Element, triangular shape, the color red)

__Love and Relationships__ – our romantic passion, love-life, and relationship with the one we hold most dear; the strength and solidity that goes along with this union (Southwest, Earth Element, square shape, the colors pink and yellow)

__Children and Creativity__ – the quality of relationships we have with our offspring, or if no children, the essence of our creative self in whatever form that may be (West, Metal Element, round, the color white)

__Helpful People__ – our "family of choice," those dearest friends who make our way smooth and with whom we share our greatest joys and most profound sorrows; in business, our clients and customers (Northwest, Metal Element, round shape, the colors gray and silver)

The colors connected with each kua relate to their general energetic association (pink for Love and Romantic Relationships) and also to the Element of that Life Aspiration (for example, yellow for Earth). The central position of the tai chi (explained further in this chapter) is tied to the Earth Element, and is also associated with the color yellow and earth tones.

You will notice that the Earth Element is found in three areas which fall in a straight line diagonally across the bagua: Love and Relationships, the tai chi, and Knowledge and Spirituality. Each Element is significant, but Earth is very important in selecting a house. Earth symbolizes a feeling of being grounded, confident, and secure — all aspects a comfortable home that will protect and nurture you. More information about the Elements is found in Chapter Five.

The Many Layers of the Bagua

The bagua is used continuously in the practice of feng shui. This energy template is "laid over" the floor plan of a structure thus placing the Life Aspiration in a physical sense within the space of a home or office. For example, when one's career is flagging and in need of greater energy, adjustments will be made in that area of the home or office that corresponds to the Career area. If healing a rift between a parent and child is in order, special energy adjustments will be applied in the Children area. If family finances are dwindling and money is continually lost, special energetic techniques will be applied to the Wealth sector.

If romance is lacking, energetic adjustments will be made in the Love and Romance area to solidify a good loving relationship, or to encourage a partner to enter one's life. If one is estranged from a particular family member, enhanced chi will be placed in the Family Life Aspiration location within the home. Especially in commercial applications, the Wealth and Helpful People (clients and customers) areas of business and office spaces are treated to large doses of continual fresh energy.

In the buying and selling of real estate, particular attention is paid to the Wealth (price of the property) and the Helpful People (buyer, seller, agents) areas of the energy template. The age-old use of the bagua is applied in countless ways to "raise" the chi where needed in order to bring balance, harmony, and good fortune into one's daily life.

Tai Chi: the Energetic Hub of the Bagua

The center of the bagua, and ninth kua, (remember the magic square with its nine numbers) is reserved for what is called the "*tai chi.*" It is often shown with a yin/yang symbol symbolizing perfect balance — the state of overall well-being. When the other eight Life Aspirations are in balance, the result is harmony and serenity in one's life, the ultimate goal of feng shui. (Have patience and you will soon see how all this relates to buying the best house for you!)

The tai chi acts like the hub of an energetic wheel that emanates from the physical center of your home or office. When the rest of the eight areas are operating at an optimum level, the central position or tai chi, will radiate the greatest beneficial energy. When applied to house floor plans, the tai chi has very important feng shui significance. Fireplaces are not recommended in the tai chi location because the all-important beneficial chi is metaphorically "burned up" and goes out the chimney.

The concepts of the lo-shu grid and the bagua are fundamental to feng shui, and are superimposed over the floor plan of a house or office space in order to position the 8 Life Aspirations. Using the bagua will be referred to often throughout this book as you apply it to various home layouts and individual rooms. Some floor plans are examples of good chi flow; others are not. One such chi challenge is a bathroom in the center (tai chi) of the floor plan.

Shown below are the Life Aspirations and tai chi of the bagua laid over a basic home floor plan. This "laying over" technique will be discussed in more detail later in this book, especially in Chapter 9. For the present, this diagram will help you to understand how the nine areas of the bagua apply to dwellings and other structures.

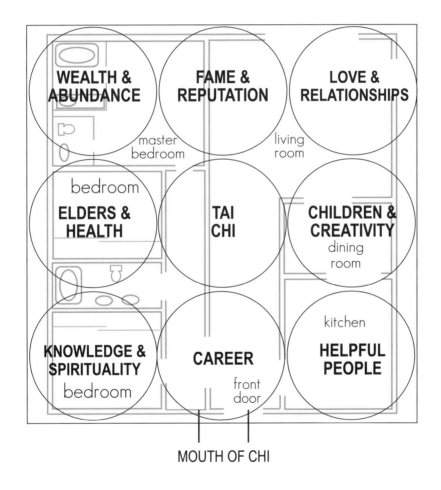

Life Aspirations and central tai chi in bagua format laid over basic floor plan.
The "Mouth of Chi" refers to the primary door.

Feng Shui — a Language of Symbols and Metaphors

As you become more familiar with the intricacies of feng shui, you will notice how symbols and metaphors play an important role in the analysis and application of feng shui guidelines. A primary example of the use of metaphor is "water" which is often called the "river of abundance."

It makes sense to have the metaphor of water equate to plenty of sustenance for the people, both from the land and from the sea; thus "wealth" is a natural result of fresh, clear, and easily flowing water. The symbolism of water, both on the land and within the structure, makes it important for water to be "held" (within the dwelling and on the site) as good energy, and not allowed to be wasted or allowed to *flow away* from the property. (*Note:* when placing fountains, be sure the water always flows inward or *toward* the dwelling.)

Fish, the wealth of the sea, are another popular example of feng shui symbolism and represent abundance (of food) and good fortune (resulting from plenty of fish to feed the people). Often the Golden Carp, which lives a long life, is designated as the primary fish symbol and can be found throughout Chinese artwork; it represents not only abundance, but also good fortune (gold) and longevity.

When you understand how important the benevolent flow of water is in feng shui, it is easy to see how seriously water is considered within a structure (and on or around the land). Any area where water leaves the house or rushes away behind the property, symbolizes the chi of abundance and good fortune draining away from the home, and therefore away from the family... not good feng shui.

A Royal Flush!

Bathrooms (and laundry rooms) obviously, are areas where water leaves the house, often through three or four drains from multiple sinks, a tub, shower, and the toilet. *The center of the home — the tai chi or energetic hub of the house — is the worst feng shui energetic location for a bathroom.* For this reason, floor plans with this condition should be passed over.

The graphic below shows how the beneficial energy of the home is sucked down and out of the house through the many drains found in bathrooms. You can see why a bathroom in the central energetic hub, the tai chi area of the home, is a major feng shui no-no.

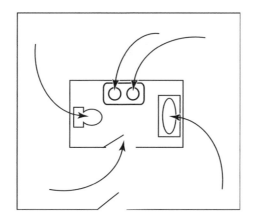

A bathroom in the central tai chi area of a home or office is best avoided.

There is a feng shui solution for this highly negative situation (Appendix C), but the reason you are reading this book is to avoid disastrous feng shui consequences in the first place, right? There are very few Feng Shui Deal Breakers™ when it comes to selecting real estate. However in this design science of symbols and metaphors, a bathroom in the center of the house would be a deal breaker. I do not take this position lightly; a bathroom in the energetic hub of a home or office will continually create financial problems and this energetic drain is very difficult and expensive to correct.

Keep the lid down to prevent the good chi of abundance from being lost.

Along this same line of thinking, you may already have read or heard that feng shui teaches that toilet lids should always be kept closed when not in use to prevent the auspicious chi from being flushed away. Knowing that water is the ultimate representation of wealth and abundance, now you understand why.

Following is a *Check Your Chi List* for this chapter that you will want to use when previewing real estate. Similar lists will be found after all chapters except Chapters 1 and 3. I call these feng shui tips "smart moves"; referring back to these basics will guide you in your real estate search. The (+) indicates a positive feng shui quality about a property, and a (-) is not a beneficial aspect. These Smart Moves Lists are compiled into a master list in the tear-out section at the back of this book that you are encouraged to photocopy and use in your selection process.

Occasionally, I rate a particular aspect of a site or house with a double minus (- -). Pay extra attention to these powerful negatives, as they are, and always will be, a BIG chi challenge for the occupants. To further help you in your home buying decision, I list the Feng Shui Deal Breakers™ in the tear-out section that are definite no-no's; be especially aware of these. Very seldom do I advise you to "get back in the car" and pass over a house, but when I do, please heed this advice.

Chapter 2 — Check Your *Chi* List

__ Analyze the energetic lines of properties contiguous to (adjoining) and across the street from the property you are considering. Are the rooflines or any other exterior element sending sha chi your way? (-)

__ Is there anything that would energetically affect your house from across the street, behind, or to the sides, such as a water tower or storage tank that is excessively high, or massive? (-)

__ Are there high power lines, transformers, ham radio antennae, a large satellite dish, or any major electric devices near your potential property? (-)

__ Is there a bathroom or laundry room located in the central tai chi area of the floor plan? (- -)

3

The Wondrous Balancing
of Yin and Yang

It has been three long months and Marcia and Nick are still looking for a new house. Nick recently retired from a large company in the Midwest and Marcia works for various nonprofit groups as a fund-raiser consultant. Adequate space for their dog, Slim, is a major factor in choosing their next home.

Marcia and Nick have already decided they want a place where each can have their own office as well as a room for guests. Both enjoy entertaining, so a great kitchen that opens to the rest of the living and family areas is very important.

Marcia and Nick have seen many houses with their broker, Chuck, who knows what they want and shows them only homes that fit their requirements, yet the ideal house has not surfaced. Because Marcia wants their next house to be their last, she is firm about her criteria.

A close friend of Marcia's has told her about feng shui guidelines to keep in mind when looking for a home. Marcia has some feng shui knowledge and appreciates its value. The house she and Nick like the best has a bathroom in the center of the house. She knows that in feng shui this type of floor plan symbolizes abundance, finances, and good fortune being energetically flushed away. She feels they need to pass on this house.

Marcia's instincts tell her to pay attention to this information, although she has not had time to study feng shui in depth. Nick has recently retired and they are now on a fixed income. As with many other investors who had a great percentage of their retirement funds in the stock market, they suffered losses, so this next housing investment has to be smart.

Chuck shows Nick and Marcia two new listings. The first one is in a nice neighborhood yet backs up to a large electric power substation — buying a home in close proximity to this excessive negative energy is out of the question. The second house is not quite as spacious as they had hoped for, though it feels wonderful to both of them. There is that special feeling of balance and serenity in this home that is lacking in the others.

Analyzing the floor plan, they see that the master bedroom is in the right, southwest rear corner, which Marcia knows is the feng shui Romance and Relationships Area; this room is especially private and pleasing. Nick's office is in the Wealth Area and gives him a feeling of peace and security. Marcia's office is in the westerly Creativity location, which is what she had hoped for. As they are sizing up the house, with the owner's permission, their dog, Slim, is playing in the large back yard.

Marcia and Nick feel "at home" in this house — they are exceptionally comfortable and at ease here. Slim is in canine heaven. As Marcia imagines having their friends over to stay in the inviting guest room, she asks Chuck, "Where do we sign?"

Universal Opposites and Complements

One of the most important feng shui concepts to understand is that of *balancing yin and yang energies within a space.* It is this principle that brings about the serenity and comfort Marcia and Nick felt, encouraging them to choose one house over others. Yin and yang are the two opposite, yet complementary, forces that operate throughout the universe. Yin represents the feminine Earth energy and yang is the masculine Heaven energy. These two energies are opposite yet equal — one cannot exist without the other. When they are in balance we feel more harmonious and serene in our homes and offices.

Feng shui teaches that the ultimate balancing of the yin and yang elements of design and color within a space benefits the flow of auspicious chi and eventually leads to a serene, comfortable, and welcoming home. It is helpful to further understand that principles found in nature are used as a guideline for the ultimate beauty, balance, and serenity.

In the yin and yang symbol, the dark portion represents the yin feminine energy and the white portion represents the yang masculine energy — all matter in the universe has a yin or a yang aspect. Yet nothing is totally yin or totally yang; their respective energies are continually replacing and replenishing each other, creating perpetual balance.

When looking at the yin and yang symbol, you will notice that there is a white yang dot in the yin black portion, and a yin black dot in the white yang area. This illustrates that even within the great warrior there exists a spark of feminine energy, such as introspective intuition or softness when it comes to children, a lover, or beloved parents.

Conversely, within even the most delicate and feminine of women there lies the power of the warrior when it comes to conviction, purpose, strength of character, or protection of one's children. Like walking a gently strung tight rope, the essence of feng shui balance is finding your true center — where you are most comfortable, and paying attention to that personal comfort zone in all your life's activities (even while you are out house hunting)! Yin and yang are not absolutes — something is yin in relation to something else that is yang — which could be yin in relationship with something else that is more yang.

Yang	**Yin**
Male	Female
Sun	Moon
Heaven	Earth
Hot	Cool
Dry	Moist
Light	Dark
Large	Small
High	Low
Hard	Soft
Sharp	Dull
Straight	Curved
Angular	Round
Plaid	Floral
Loud	Quiet

Examples of Yin and Yang Universal Opposites

Everyone has personal preferences about their comfort zone — the kind of climate and environment where they would most like to live. Even though some people prefer a hot, yang climate, there are times when they will come out of the sun and seek the yin shade. Those who find it most comfortable living in a cool yin forest location will still look for sunny yang days when they can be outside without a jacket. We all have our unique ideas about what is the ideal spot for us when it comes to climate and our happiest environment.

Some yin and yang examples of site selection (location) are:

<u>**Yin**</u>	<u>**Yang**</u>
valley	mountain top
small town	large city
quiet street	bustling neighborhood
forest	desert
shady side of street	bright, sunny exposure
single level	high-rise condominium
small square footage	large, expansive in size
house sits back away from street	directly on a main avenue

Remember that the goal of feng shui is balance. You can have a smaller, single level home in a large city on the shady side of the street, in a quiet neighborhood. If your job dictates that you live in a large metropolis, you can balance that massive, yang energy by choosing a yin setting.

As feng shui relates to real estate and the *interior* of houses, the balance between yin and yang refers to:

- ☯ finding shade within our homes in a hot climate, and reaching for the light of the sun in a cool, shady climate by using skylights and large windows.

- ☯ where the various rooms are placed in the house in relation to the street and main entrance (yang rooms toward the street and yin rooms to the rear of the house).

- ☯ structural angles and curves. (Look for rounded shapes such as arches and arched windows, lacy foliage that softens the hard edges of most house designs.)

- ☯ appropriate use of yin and yang colors for the specific purposes and functions of the living spaces. Bright, warm colors in yang rooms and cooler shades in yin areas.

Public Spaces and Private Places — Yin & Yang Functioning Rooms

Each room has a yin or a yang function. Ask yourself, "Is the purpose of this room *yin* — one for rest and quiet (such as a bedroom)?" or "Is this space for *yang* activities (the kitchen or family room)?" After deciding which rooms are devoted to yin or yang functions, determine approximately where the home's mid-line is in relation to the street. *Yang rooms are best placed toward the front of the house toward the street and traffic; yin rooms are ideally positioned toward the rear where the energy is quiet and protected.*

For example, living rooms, family rooms, dining rooms, and kitchens are all yang rooms. They are rather public in nature, and the energy found there is active. Ideally these rooms should be in *front of the home's mid-line.*

Bedrooms, especially the master bedroom, other bedrooms, the office, study, and library are yin functioning rooms. They are private in nature; the energy there is quiet, relaxing, and intended to renew the spirit. Optimum feng shui positioning for these rooms is in the rear of the house, *behind the mid-line.*

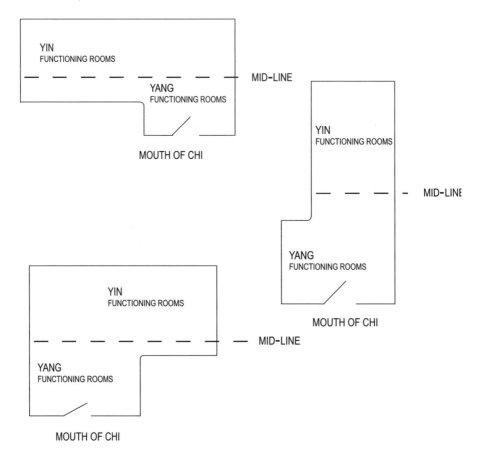

Floor plans showing house mid-line. Front door (mouth of chi) and ideally yang rooms are closest to the street and traffic energy.

Ruby Slippers, Take Me to My Comfort Zone

Why do we feel more "at home" in one place than in another? Conversely, why do we want to get up and escape as soon as possible in other houses? As you search for the ideal home, pay close attention to your feelings, that "inner barometer" that whispers happy and comforting words as you find your special place.

Each of us has this unique "comfort zone" — our own sweet spot, an environment where we feel most at home and at peace. For some it will be in the desert, for others it is within a shaded forest or in the mountains. For most of us it will be somewhere in the middle, a more easily attainable setting that speaks to our souls.

Not everyone can afford exactly the ideal setting they would like, so our landscaping and dwelling can mimic or re-create as closely as possible our heart's desire. Like Dorothy trying to get back to her beloved home in Kansas, we need to click the heels of our energetic ruby slippers, and keep looking until we find that special place where we are able to re-create the environment that most closely touches the special place that makes our inner heart smile.

This Magic Moment

When real estate professionals show property to clients and finally arrive at that ultimate home, they notice that buyers often do not talk very much; they just walk around smiling. At this point, an experienced agent will not break the spell with excess talk or questions. At the perfect house, few words are necessary.

This is when the buyers are bonding with the home on an inner, subtle, energetic level. The buyers will break the silence with comments about how they will place furnishings, by asking questions about how soon the sellers will move, and by letting the agent know they are ready to write an offer.

But buyers watch out! When this magic moment arrives you will hopefully have finished reading this book and will have done your *Feng Shui Property Appraisal™* (found in Chapter 6) on other properties you have previewed so that by now it's easy to discern which properties have good feng shui! You want this spell of delight to last a long time and to be certain this is the most auspicious house for you.

In Chapter 6, I explain how to go about checking out all the feng shui details. To further assist you, the tear-out sheets at the back of this book give you a master *Check Your Chi List* of feng shui "smart moves" to use with each property you are serious about. This, in addition to the *Feng Shui Property Appraisal™*, are all you will need to evaluate the properties you preview. *Do not forget to complete this simple Feng Shui Property Appraisal™ before you make an offer.* My goal is to have extremely happy buyers, certain you have chosen the energetically right house, making you joyful for years to come!

Yin & Yang — Vivé la Différence!

Besides the placement of yin- and yang-functioning rooms, the principle of balancing yin and yang *shapes* and *angles* enters the picture. Even more balance can be found in a structure that has an equilibrium among its angular yang corners and linear yang elements (beams and posts) and its yin rounded or softened shapes such as arched windows.

More and more frequently we see architects using arched windows in a residential design. This shift away from the traditional 90 degree cornered windows gives a refreshing yin break from the typical yang shapes. Often within meditation spaces or garden areas devoted to contemplation we will find a round or "moongate" window or entry. This yin application of shape brings such a beautiful balance to otherwise harsh yang corners that it makes us stop for a moment to appreciate the loveliness.

The round (yin) mirror beautifully balances the 90 degree (yang) angles of the fireplace and mantle. Photo: Anne Czajka

Recently, I visited Fess Parker's *DoubleTree Inn* in Santa Barbara, California, where the architect has done a masterful job of balancing yin and yang shapes within the grand foyer and lobby.

The grand lobby of Fess Parker's DoubleTree Hotel, Santa Barbara, California, displays excellent balance of yin and yang shapes.

The gentle curves of the large arched doors and windows take the "yang" edge off the normal 90 degree angles of corners and furniture. The interior spaces are defined by curving short walls and staircases that gracefully sweep upward. A stunning bagua-shaped octagonal skylight floods the interior with welcoming natural sunshine, and a wall of water panels cascades into a waiting pool along the south entrance. Absolutely great feng shui!

As you analyze various homes for sale, begin to assess the many 90-degree yang angles within each room versus rounded yin shapes.

Begin thinking how you will balance all these angles with softening draperies, gently rounded upholstered furniture, circular or oval area rugs, picture frames with gently rounded corners, etc. This is where the creative fun of feng shui comes in!

Color Me Yin or Yang

Besides yin and yang aspects of shapes and angles, there is a yin and yang quality to the colors surrounding us. The yin side of the color wheel is the area of cool colors: blue, green, lavender, gray, and black. The yang colors are on the warm side of the color wheel: red, orange, yellow, brown, and earth tones.

When working with yin and yang colors, we work with *tints*, *tones*, and *shades*. Colors that can be softened into a yin color by adding white are referred to as *tints* — with enough white added, red becomes light petal pink. A *tone* is a color to which gray or some of the complement of the hue has been added — the result is one of the many colors of brown. A *shade* is a hue to which black has been added to darken the original color into more of a yin color.

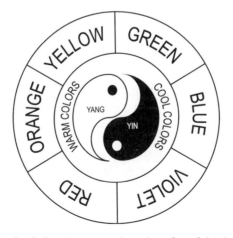

Color wheel showing warm (yang) and cool (yin) colors.

When decorating the spaces within our homes and offices, yin functioning rooms (bedrooms, bathrooms, the private office) would be appropriately done in yin hues — blues, greens, and lavenders, with touches of warm yang colors for accents. For color in yang functioning rooms such as the kitchen, living room, family room, dining area, and an office space where clients visit, use warm yang colors that are more appropriate for higher energy spaces.

When too much of a yang color (red for example) is used in a yin space (a bedroom), the occupant will not feel much like resting. If a yang room such as a kitchen is colored in yin shades (deep blue, dark green, purple), quiet restful energy will prevail.

The *Madonna Inn*, in San Luis Obispo, California is famous for its "Madonna pink" décor found throughout the entire hotel, from the coffee shop with its copper tabletops, to the elaborately decorated restrooms. Everywhere one finds pink napkins, tablecloths, wallpaper, and rose-festooned carpeting. From towering, boulder-lined pathways, and multi-colored lighted fountains, guests enter through massive double doors into an array of fairyland lights.

The Madonna Inn, San Luis Obispo, California

This landmark hotel is the epitome of yang energy; light and vibrant colors have been splashed everywhere with great results. The Madonna Inn is a showplace and, over the decades, locals and guests of all ages have come happily flocking again and again to the place where the yang energy lifts their spirits and provides a background for eating, dancing, and playing.

These two commercial examples of applying yin and yang shapes and colors show, on a commercial scale, how these design elements can be effectively used in a residential setting. Do not hesitate to have fun with yin and yang aspects of shape and color to create balance within your home.

The Real Estate Power Positions

Gina and Dave know every house in town that is on the market; they are thorough and check everything that hits the papers. Dave is an expert cement contractor and runs his business from home — his office is critically important to him. Gina is a medical technician and when she finishes work she wants to relax; gourmet cooking is her specialty and she loves working in her garden.

Jeanne Marie, their real estate agent, is also very thorough. She seems to know what properties are coming on the market before the newspaper does, and has been using all her skills to find Gina and Dave the right house. She makes appointments to preview new listings, then she shows Gina and Dave only the properties that meet their specifications.

Gina arranges to be off early from work and they all set off to look at homes Monday afternoon. The first house is in a great location, yet has a severe slope in the back of the property that bothers Dave; walking out to the rear of the lot, Dave feels as though the back yard is falling off a cliff. The house is okay and Gina likes the kitchen. In the room he would use for his office, the only place a desk will fit puts Dave with his back to the door

— he is uncomfortable with this arrangement. Any other furniture placement would eliminate his credenza and bookcase. Either way he is not thrilled.

The next house is on a cul-de-sac, but only a short way inside the closed street. It is a quiet neighborhood and Gina especially likes the beautiful trees that surround the properties on the street. The master bedroom is serene and allows them to place their bed so they can face the door diagonally. Dave's desk will have plenty of room so he can put his desk and chair in his first Best Direction. This house is looking good.

In the kitchen, Gina is pleased that she can cook without having her back to the door; she dislikes feeling like she is missing the activity in the rest of the room. The natural light is wonderful and Gina can see her garden from where she prepares their food. The great room is perfect and their front door faces what her feng shui book says is her "Best Direction." Both Gina and Dave are excited about this house.

It does not take them long to decide they should submit an offer for this property. After their long wait, this house has a majority of the things they are hoping to find. Dave and Gina are smiling and mentally already moving in. Jeanne Marie is determined to get this offer accepted. She is smiling too.

Many of the factors Gina and Dave have looked for in their new house have to do with, what in feng shui is called, the "command" or "power" position. This chapter focuses on this important concept on the macro level for the site of the overall property, and on the micro level of furniture placement within significant rooms of the house. The "command" position is fundamental to feng shui analysis; its importance should not be overlooked when looking for real estate.

The "Armchair" Site for Homes

The *armchair* location refers to the placement of a structure on the land. The *command position* relates to the interior positioning of furniture in a room. Both the armchair position and the command position are power positions. We will first discuss the exterior application of the feng shui power position. The metaphor of the "armchair position" originated early in feng shui history (refer to Chapter 1) and shows how best to position cities, palaces, temples, and ultimately, dwellings. You will want to give the armchair position consideration when previewing potential homes.

Recall that feng shui began with the auspicious placement of grave sites. It became evident that when a building was placed within the protected and nurtured "belly of the dragon," the site proved to be especially fortunate. On either side of the dwelling, as in an armchair, there are elements of energetic support and protection.

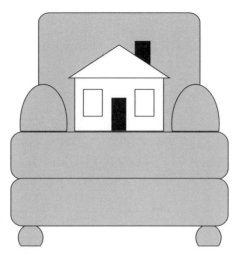

*Ideal Position for House Sitting Approximately 1/3 of the Way
from the Top of the (Armchair) Hill*

Frank Lloyd Wright's now famous mountain homes were never built at the tops of hills. He much preferred locations slightly downhill, usually about 20 percent away from the peak. He said he did not like to put a building, like a hat, on the top of a mountain; rather he preferred "to add an eyebrow on the mountain."[3] This world-renowned architect was practicing "intuitive" feng shui. He knew that although a home, office, or a temple would have a great view at the top of a hill, hilltop building sites came at a price — the price of the owner's physical and energetic comfort.

But remember, feng shui is all about balance and living in harmony with the natural environment. When the "feng" wind comes too harshly it disturbs our inner chi; it makes us feel uncomfortable, unable to enjoy the outside beauty, and we are driven indoors. Then we close the doors and windows and take shelter from the storm. In feng shui, the top of a

[3] *Feng Shui — How to Achieve the Most Harmonious Arrangement of Your Home and Office*, Angel Thompson, p. 60.

hill or mountain is referred to as the "head of the dragon" and as such is an energetically precarious house location.

The ideal position for a dwelling site is between one-fifth to one-third of the way down a hill, with more gentle hillocks or trees on either side, and with a view of a waterway to the front. Ocean view property anyone? This is the ideal... it is not always achievable or affordable, but try to get as many of these feng shui supportive features as possible in your next investment.

Home in the classic feng shui "armchair" position.

Unconditional Support

To maximize the beneficial effects of the armchair position, the site should have *support at the rear and sides of the property* — a mountain or hill, tall trees or shrubs, a strong wall or sturdy high fence, rocks or boulders... things that provide physical and energetic protection.

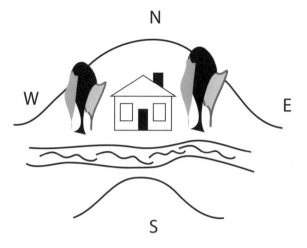

Feng shui armchair position applied to home site.

Avoid parcels that slope down in the rear. Lots with this topography allow the chi of abundance and fortunate blessings to drain easily and quickly away from the parcel. They do not give the necessary energetic support from behind.

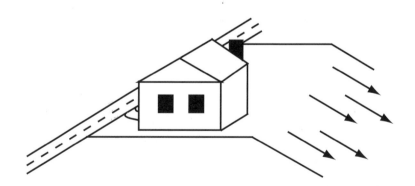

A parcel sloping down to the rear allows beneficial chi to drain away.

These lots can be remedied by planting fast-growing substantial trees, placing boulders at the crest of the slope, or both. Though it is better feng shui to avoid these parcels; I once lived on a property with a rear slope and planted liquid amber trees along the rim of the slope to add to the needed protection.

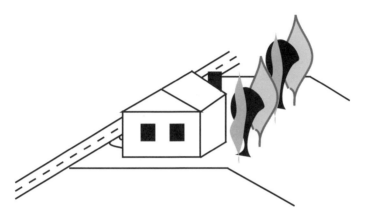

Trees or strong energetic elements such as a hill, wall, or fence will "hold" the chi in place.

Look for property that has trees or tall, healthy shrubs on either side of the house. The feng shui symbology is the Green Dragon to the left as you look out (East) and the White Tiger to the right (West) as is explained in Chapter 1. The energy of the dragon should dominate slightly over the tiger, so the trees or foliage to the left side of the house (looking out) can be slightly taller. The trees or shrubs on both sides may be shorter than the rear landscaping and can taper toward the front. These elements will provide energetic support and will be an excellent privacy screen between you and your side neighbors.

Fences and walls work too, but remember Robert Frost's admonition in his poem, *Mending Wall*:

> *Before I built a wall I'd ask to know*
> *What I was walling in or walling out,*
> *And to whom I was like to give offence.*
> *Something there is that doesn't love a wall,*
> *That wants it down.*

For a more natural, and many think a more inviting division, avoid fences and walls and use natural elements such as trees or shrubs between properties. However, in today's world of backyard dogs, a wall may be necessary. Perhaps a short wall will suffice with planted shrubs to camouflage unforgiving brick and mortar.

Jesse Always Faced the Door

In addition to the classic feng shui armchair position of a homesite, another position on the interior that gives energetic support and empowers the owner of a home is the "command" or power position. This concept is used *within any significant room* of a house such as the master bedroom, kitchen, office, and living room.

Think of Jesse James who would not be caught dead with his back to the door. Facing the door, preferably with a wall at your back, gives you an energetic feng shui ace in your hand — meaning additional self-confidence and a feeling of being in control. Who would not want more of that? For the best feng shui, you want to *face the door, but not look directly out the door.*

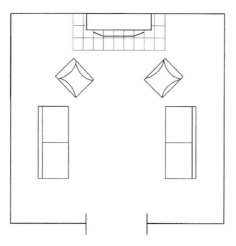

Example of living room furniture command placement so that all seating is able to view the door (or the entrance) to the room.

In China, the mistress and master of the house are always given the position of utmost respect and would therefore assume the command position at the dinner table or in the living room. *Try to place yourself in the area of greatest protection with support from behind.* This means having a wall behind you, not a window. When you are in the command position you feel capable, focused, in control, and decisive. You should determine whether or not your furniture will fit to give you the command position in the following rooms:

- ☯ master bedroom as you sleep

- ☯ kitchen as you cook and prepare food

- ☯ office where you sit at your desk and make business decisions

- ☯ living room where your favorite chair is placed

- ☯ dining area where you sit at the table for meals

- ☯ other bedrooms for children and guests as they sleep

Most Important: the Master Bedroom

As the most yin room in the house where owners spend one-third of their lives, the master bedroom is considered the most important area for feng shui placement. As already discussed, this special room should be at the rear of the house, definitely behind the mid-line, preferably in the far right or southwest corner because this is the Romance Life Aspiration of the bagua. Having the master bedroom in this location is especially auspicious and portends a solid, loving relationship.

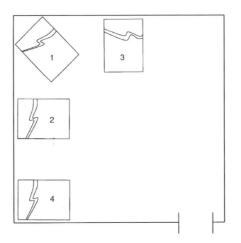

Examples of Good Feng Shui Bed Placement

Note: Placing the bed diagonally in a corner location may give you a strong position, but will need a substantial headboard; a plant or other grounding element will fill that space and help avoid negative chi behind the bed.

Additionally, in your new home, be sure that the master bed can be placed in such a way that your feet are not pointing out the door. Referred to as the "coffin position," this is a big feng shui no-no, as it is the position the dead are carried out of a room! Place the bed so that you see the door, yet do not look directly out the door.

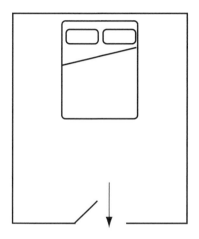

Bed in the "Coffin Position"

Unfortunately, this is sometimes the only way a bed can be positioned because of closets, windows, and door placement. This is an energetically poor location for any bed, but the master bed especially should not be put in this spot. Serious students of feng shui would find another solution: turning this room into an office or weight room, making it into a craft space, television or game room. They would find an alternative space where the bed would have a more auspicious location, and would not sleep, or have their children sleep, with their feet pointing out the door.

Recipe for Success — *Command* the Kitchen

After the master bedroom, the kitchen is considered to be the most important room for feng shui placement. Further application of the command position is focused here. If at all possible, it is very auspicious if the cook faces the door (but does not look directly out the door) when at the stove. This keeps the cook energetically satisfied, happy, and comfortable while preparing food for the family.

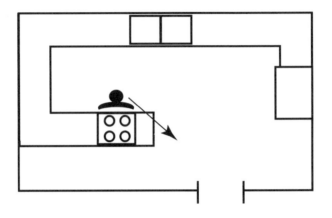

Good Feng Shui Command Position for Kitchen Stove

As a strong Fire Element (explained in Chapter 5) and symbol of prosperity, the stove placement is best kept away from the Water Element of the sink. If the sink (especially in a small kitchen) is directly across from the stove, the Fire and Water Elements are in "energetic conflict." This situation can be mitigated by hanging a faceted crystal between the two elements. Because of the energetic symbolism of waste water, it is also recommended that an upper floor bathroom not be positioned directly above the stove. The kitchen is where the family nourishment is prepared and the stove is a significant metaphor for the blessings, health, and good fortune that affect every member of the household.

If the cook must face a wall, sometimes a mirror or other reflective surface is recommended above the stove to help the cook see what is going on behind them. If you implement this solution, be sure that the mirror is hung high enough to reflect as much of the upper body and head of the cook as possible, so as not to distort reality.

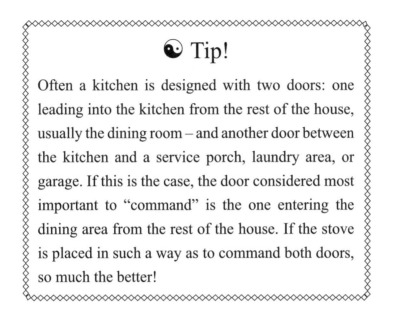

☯ Tip!

Often a kitchen is designed with two doors: one leading into the kitchen from the rest of the house, usually the dining room – and another door between the kitchen and a service porch, laundry area, or garage. If this is the case, the door considered most important to "command" is the one entering the dining area from the rest of the house. If the stove is placed in such a way as to command both doors, so much the better!

Since You Are the Boss, Check out the Office

As you preview property, analyze the possible furniture placement in the room you are considering for your office. Try to place your desk so that, when sitting in your chair, you can easily see the door without craning your neck or looking over your shoulder to see who comes in or passes by in the hallway.

A feng shui energetic bonus in the office is a solid wall behind your chair for energetic support. A window for natural light and ventilation is also highly desirable. However, it is *not advisable* to have the window directly behind your chair, as the all-important chi tends to fall through the fragile window instead of staying inside to support you. Also be sure that any filing cabinet or bookcase behind your chair does not produce a sha arrow pointing at your back.

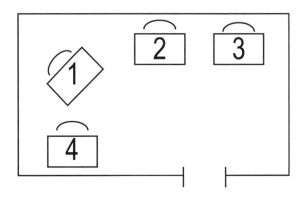

Desk Possibilities in Order of their Good Feng Shui Position

You need enough room around your desk for the chi to move freely. Bookcases, credenzas, filing cabinets, computer tables, or other equipment that you use often should all be within easy reach so you do not have to leave your chair. You want convenience without constricting your own chi.

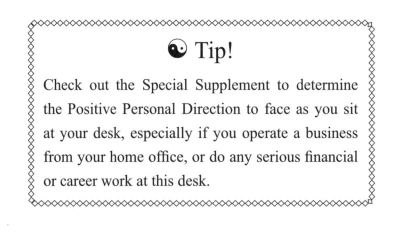

☯ Tip!

Check out the Special Supplement to determine the Positive Personal Direction to face as you sit at your desk, especially if you operate a business from your home office, or do any serious financial or career work at this desk.

Dine the Feng Shui Way

When considering the command position of the various rooms in the house, also check out the dining room. While this is not the most critical area for many buyers, to those who entertain often and have frequent parties and guests, the dining room is significant.

Remember that the whole idea of the command position is to give the mistress and master of the home a greater feeling of confidence, energetic support, and a sense of being grounded — all important considerations when hosting a party! Again, where is the door?

As the primary maestro orchestrating your dinner parties, think about where you will sit. *The command position is not necessarily at the head of the table, but rather the spot that allows you to most easily see the door.* Try to place the table so you can do both — and face one of your Best Directions! (See Special Supplement)

As is often the case with the kitchen, there may be more than one door leading into the dining room. If so, try to command the entrance where guests will most frequently enter and leave – if you can also see the door where the food is brought in from the kitchen that is an added plus.

Just be sure there is not a kitchen door directly behind or too close to where you are sitting. This entry will be constantly filled with too much active and distracting chi. Try to have this service passageway as far from you as possible, unless of course you are doing all the serving.

Chapter 4— Check Your *Chi* List

___ Does the property have some energetically supportive feature at the back such as a hill, healthy trees, tall shrubs, or a solid fence or wall? (+)

___ Does the parcel have some sort of protective foliage, or at least strong fencing, on either side of the house? (+)

___ Does the property slope down and away from the house in the rear? (-)

___ Is there a lower area of land out to the front that gives a distant, pleasing view? (+)

___ Will you be able to place the master bed so that you are in the command position? (+)

___ Does the bed placement allow you to sleep facing (with your head pointing toward) one of your Best Directions? (+)

___ Is the master bedroom in the far right rear corner or Southwest area of the house? (+)

___ Can you face the main kitchen door when cooking? (+)

___ Is the stove close to or directly across from the sink? (-)

___ Is there enough room for good chi circulation around your desk and office furniture? (+)

___ Does the floor plan allow your desk and chair to command the door? (+)

___ Will your office chair be able to face at least one of your Positive Personal Directions? (+)

___ Is there a window behind where you will place your desk (-) or a solid wall? (+)

___ If entertaining is important to you, will your dining table placement allow you to be seated in the command position and still be far enough away from the distracting energy of the kitchen door? (+)

___ Do the seating positions allow you to face one of your Best Personal Directions when dining? (+)

The Magic of the
Five Elements

Jackie and Jim have 60 days to find a new house. Their condo has sold and the buyers have put down a large deposit. Now the clock is ticking for them to get busy with their agent, Judy, and see what is on the market in their price range.

The first house Judy shows them is spotless and well cared for, yet feels formal and rigid. Everything is painted white and has metal design treatments throughout. Jim and Jackie have a one year old baby girl and know the next house for them will need to be comfortable and more on the informal side.

The next house is beautiful with lush plants and a great back yard; they can hear the sound of a waterfall just outside the dining room. However, the owners have painted the interior a soft blue and have just installed intense blue plush carpeting. Jim mentions that he feels like he is having to walk on water in this house. Jackie feels cold here and knows they want a warm, sunny house.

The third house has natural wood paneling throughout. When they open all the blinds, the outside foliage feels like it is climbing inside. The new carpeting and linoleum are hunter green. This place feels like a tree house. Determined not to get discouraged, they decide to keep looking.

The next house Judy shows them has a big porch and a sunlit entry. The living room and dining area have wood paneling halfway up the walls. There is a large brick fireplace and several picture windows that fill the entire front of the house with light. A big mirror above the dining table reflects a lush view from the opposite window. The carpeting is a rich champagne beige that will go with any color scheme, and the kitchen has large paver tiles.

Jackie and Jim are smiling as they continue through the house into the bedrooms. French doors lead out from the master suite to an inviting deck filled with pots of colorful flowers and a spa. The baby's room is large enough so that she can enjoy the space while growing. The two other bedrooms are ideal for a guest room and an office.

Jackie and Jim grin at each other and know they do not have to look any further. They ask Judy to write the full price offer at the dining table instead of going back to the office; they want to stay and enjoy this special house a while longer.

The Language of the Five Elements —
Now You Are Talking Feng Shui!

In their search for the home where they feel most comfortable, Jackie and Jim are responding to imbalances of the Five Elements in the first three houses. The first home was overweighted toward the Element Metal – rigid and formal. The second was overboard with the Water Element, and the third had too much of the Wood Element. Without knowing why, they loved the house that was energetically balanced with all Five Elements.

In addition to knowing the concept of chi, balancing yin and yang, using the bagua, and understanding the use of the command position, another important component of feng shui comes into prominent play — the *interaction of the Five Elements: Water, Wood, Fire, Earth, and Metal*. The Five Elements have associated colors, shapes, and directions (used in Compass School).

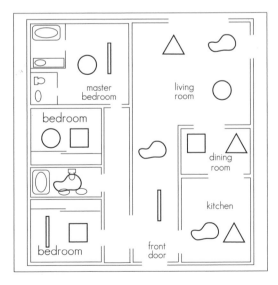

A well balanced house has a balanced distribution of all Five Elements.

Element	Color	Shape	Direction
Water	Black, Deep Blue	Amorphous, ellipse, Paisley	North
Wood	Green, Blue-Green	Column, Tree Shape	East & Southeast
Fire	Red, Burgundy	Pyramid, Triangle, Flame	South
Earth	Yellow, Ochre, Earth Tones	Square	Northeast & Southeast
Metal	White, Gray, Silver	Circle	West

The Five Elements Chart

Chi and yin/yang comprise the vocabulary for the rich language of feng shui; the lo shu magic square and the bagua provide the sentence structure, and the Five Element Theory is the grammar that glues the entire energetic package together. When you understand this language, your feng shui skills will be honed to a new and higher dimension — that of Elemental balance.

Without having some understanding of the Five Elements, you are practicing feng shui with one hand tied behind your back; you are at a distinct disadvantage. Do not worry, the Elemental water is warm, fun, and inviting! So it makes sense to roll up your energetic sleeves and dive in.

The Five Elements — Water, Wood, Fire, Earth, and Metal — are an additional and profound layer that empowers you to put feng shui into immediate action in your home or office space. Placement of Elemental design appointments can be the best way to bring a space into true energetic balance and make the area feel welcoming and serene.

As we live and work, the balance of these Five Elements (or lack of it) affects us on a subtle, energetic level. When all the Elements are in harmony within a space, we feel comfortable and welcomed — we want to stay. If there is an imbalance among any of the Elements, or if one of the Elements is missing, we feel uncomfortable and energetically out of sorts. We can not quite put our finger on what is the problem, but our subtle anatomy knows something is not in harmony.

Your Five Element Tool Box

The chi of all matter can be assigned to one or more of the Five Elements.
These aspects of energy characterize every substance, living or inert.
Examples follow throughout this chapter that will give you ideas for Five
Element usage that you can put to practice immediately in your current
home or office, and certainly keep in mind when house hunting.

When you understand how to work with the Five Elements to achieve
balance, you will have a new toolbox to design houses and landscapes
(and even select furniture) that will allow you to create spaces that feel
alive and serene at the same time.

The Five Elements and their characteristics are:

Water

Shape:	amorphous, pond shape, paisley, amoeba-like
Color:	blue, black, deep green, ocean colors
Direction:	North
Examples:	pictures of the ocean, fish, lake scenes, mirrors, glass, any shimmering texture
Found In:	any water feature or reflective surface, fountain, aquarium, shells
Personality:	flexible and open minded, introspective and creative
Life Aspiration:	Career

Wood

Shape:	columnar, tree trunk-like, vertical shapes
Color:	all shades of green
Direction:	East, Southeast
Examples:	wood furniture, paneling, picture frames, wood flooring, grasscloth wallpaper, floral prints, silk, cotton, linen
Found In:	live plants, vibrant silk plants, pictures of forests, still lifes, beams, posts, all vertical design elements, and plaids

Personality:	creative and inspirational, filled with new ideas
Life Aspiration:	Family and Elders, Wealth

Fire

Shape:	triangular, pyramid, flame shape
Color:	red in all shades, flame hues
Direction:	South
Examples:	lighting, fireplace, stove, candles, Southwest prints
Found In:	pictures of people, pets, wildlife, or paintings predominated by or matted with red, fur, animal prints
Personality:	passionate, exuberant, filled with enthusiasm
Life Aspiration:	Fame

Earth

Shape:	square and rectangle
Color:	yellows, ochre shades, all browns and earth tones
Direction:	Southwest, Northeast
Examples:	scenes of mountains, plains, deserts, fields
Found In:	stucco, adobe, tile, brick, ceramic, porcelain, terra cotta, or any porous, loamy-type earth material
Personality:	grounded, solid, confident, steadfast, and nurturing
Life Aspiration:	Love Relationships, Knowledge and Wisdom

Metal

Shape:	circle, oval, arch
Color:	white, silver, gray, metallic tones, jewel colors
Direction:	West, Northwest
Examples:	metal sculpture, metal picture frames, brass planters, circular furniture shapes
Found In:	metal and ores of all types, silver, brass, pewter, chrome, granite, marble, precious and semi-precious stones
Personality:	mental focus, acuity, determination, strength of purpose
Life Aspiration:	Children and Creativity, Helpful People

It Is All in the Balance

The Five Elements act together to create, control, and reduce each other according to the cycles described below. I encourage you to become familiar with these cycles, the characteristics of the Elements and practice identifying them as you preview houses for purchase.

Paying attention to this important layer of feng shui will be the icing on the energetic recipe you are preparing, and your final product will be delicious! Remember that the goal of learning and using this exciting dimension of the Five Elements is *balance* within a space. The ideal is to have all the Elements represented on your property:

- ☯ the *overall land* (trees, colorful plants, statuary, benches, gazing balls, fountains, arbors, gates, etc.) pathways

- ☯ the *physical structure* of the house or commercial building (roof design, columns at the front, shapes of windows, shutters, window boxes, etc.)

- ☯ the *rooms* within the house (design appointments throughout, paneling, lighting, windows, mirrors, furniture, artwork, flooring, wall colors, ceiling treatments, etc.)

You want to understand and be able to identify various aspects of the Five Elements as you analyze and select real estate because this information will fine tune the way in which you view (and ultimately select) property. For example, if you preview a home that really appeals to you and has basically good feng shui, however the over abundance of 90 degree angles and pointy corners throughout needs to be mitigated.

You can plan how you will soften and help these yang angles so that the space will feel more balanced with the help of yin window treatments, plants, colors, and design appointments. You will know that your furnishings will need to be on the yin side: upholstered furniture with rounded corners and round or oval tables instead of square ones.

Front porches usually are filled with yang 90 degree angles when you begin to look with your new feng shui eyes. The door, windows, roof corners, square pillars, all have yang corners. This situation can easily be balanced with round color bowls of blooming plants, an oval or semi-circular door mat, porch light with a round design instead of a square one, soft fabric window treatments that show from the outside, instead of rigid, linear mini-blinds.

Working with All Five Elements

As you pursue your new home selection, you want to balance and harmonize each of the Five Elements on a parcel, within a structure, and inside the rooms. When you achieve "balance" within a space you are dealing with weight, volume, and mass. When you are bringing "harmony" into an area you are working with placement and distribution of Elements. You can accomplish both balance and harmony by incorporating the:

- *Element itself* (wood paneling, metal light fixtures, terra cotta paver tiles, a table fountain, a fireplace)

- *Energetic shape* associated with each Element (a circular coffee table, arched doorways, an oval window in a front door, all from the Metal Element.)

- *Symbolic color* of each Element (area carpets with red hues, burgundy throw pillows on a bed or sofa, red matting around a painting, red candles, a red gazing ball in the garden are all symbolic of the Fire Element.)

The Nourishing Cycle

It is easier to understand how the Five Elements work in a cycle to nourish each other when they are arranged in a *clockwise* formation. In the **Nourishing Cycle** — Water nourishes Wood; Wood feeds Fire; Fire creates Earth (ash); Earth creates Metal (ore, jewels); and Metal holds Water. This cycle shows you what Element to add (to feed or nourish) to a poorly represented Element in order to raise its energy.

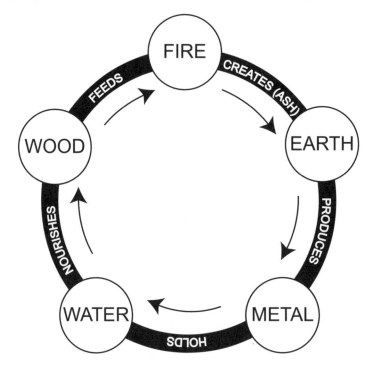

The Nourishing Cycle of the Elements

For example, if you want to accentuate the Element of Water in the entry way (Career area) of a floor plan because you are starting a new line of work, first use an abundance of the Water Element such as a black or deep blue area rug, a seascape, or an arrangement of shells on a side entry table. Then use Metal to nourish (hold) the Water Element. A metal frame around a painting of the sea, a metal table fountain, or a metal bowl holding water with floating flowers in the central front of the house would all be easy Elemental ways to raise the chi to energetically bolster your new career.

The Controlling Cycle

The next cycle is the **Controlling Cycle** — Water extinguishes Fire; Fire melts Metal; Metal cuts Wood; Wood displaces Earth (as in tree roots); and Earth dams Water.

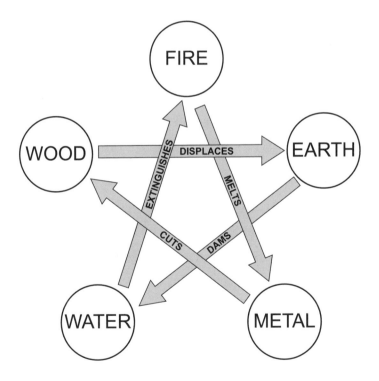

The Controlling Cycle of the Elements

The Controlling Cycle does exactly what you might expect — tones down or controls an excess of one or more of the Five Elements. For example, if you have too much of the Wood Element in a room, you would use the Metal Element to control the Wood. Brass planters, a round coffee table, a white shawl draped over a sofa, and white walls all add the Metal Element to "cut" the excess of Wood.

Use of the Controlling Cycle will suppress an overabundance of any particular Element with its controlling partner. For example: a living room painted white, with metal picture frames, a metal coffee table, a white sofa, and white carpeting, would be out of balance elementally toward Metal. The room would feel rigid and unyielding, and not allow you to energetically relax.

To help balance this room, use Metal's controlling element of Fire. Incorporate design appointments with Fire energy such as a burgundy area rug under the coffee table, burgundy throw pillows on the sofa, brick red mats around paintings or pictures on the walls, and red candles throughout the room. These Fire Elements will "control" the excess Metal.

The Reduction Cycle

The next cycle is the **Reduction Cycle**. Think of this approach as reducing the power of an Element, not destroying or controlling it. To accomplish this reduction process, reverse the Nourishing Cycle and go *counter-clockwise* around the circle of Elements. For example: Earth will extinguish Fire; Fire will burn Wood; Wood will deplete Water (through roots); Water will dissolve minerals (Metal); and Metal (a shovel) will reduce Earth.

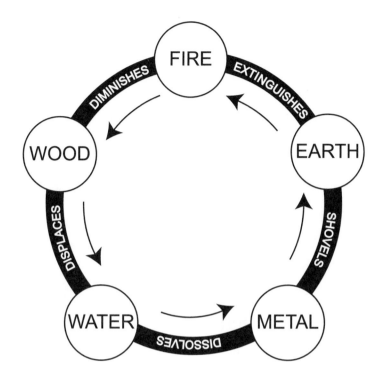

The Reduction Cycle of the Elements

The three Elemental cycles work together to help balance the Five Elements within any home or environment. Using each cycle independently will help you bring Elemental balance into any space. The more you practice identifying and recognizing the Five Elements, the more skilled you will become at this very effective method of bringing greater harmony and balance within any space.

Use of Elemental Colors

The Five Elements are especially useful when assigning color to various rooms within a home or office.

Earth: yellow, ochres, brown, all earth tones

Metal: white, grey, silver, metallic tones

Water: blue, black, water hues

Wood: green of all shades

Fire: red in all shades, flame tones

When you want to achieve balance within a space, it is easy to add the color of the Element that is missing, or under-represented. If a garden needs more of the Fire Element, choose plants that blossom red, such as bougainvillea, poinsettia, or red azaleas. To further enhance the Fire Element, according to the Nourishing Cycle, you can "feed" fire by adding the Wood Element. Evergreen plants, and all green shrubs will do the trick. Wood benches, a green gazing ball, or a green banner all accomplish the same goal.

Note: Different schools of feng shui differ on the directions associated with the Five Elements. (Black Sect does not use traditional compass directions.) Do not worry about this lack of agreement for our purpose of buying real estate. I will refer to the Five Elements throughout this text, especially in conjunction with balancing colors, shapes, textures, to achieve harmony, tranquility, and well-being for all areas of a property.

When you do not feel particularly comfortable inside a house or you sense an imbalance in a particular room, do a "Five Elements check." Determine which Elements are overly abundant, or lacking altogether. The rooms where your chi responds with "dis-ease" are those where one Element dominates to the exclusion of one or several others. Usually we find Wood and Earth to be more than sufficiently represented in wooden furniture and stucco wallboard construction. Most often Water or Metal is lacking.

Sometimes Water is too abundant. Real estate agents are familiar with the listing with the blue carpeting and soft blue walls — the one that is hard to sell. People who love blue are passionate about the color and use it everywhere. The rest of the buying public like blue well enough, they just don't want it everywhere. There is an Elemental reason for this: blue carpeting is a metaphor for the Water Element. To have a home carpeted in blue makes us feel "wishy-washy" and as though we are trying to "walk on water." We would prefer something more solid and "grounded" such as Earth or Wood.

Mobile Homes Are Predominantly Metal

Most mobile homes are constructed of a wood frame wrapped in metal siding, so they are heavily weighted toward the Metal Element. An excess of Metal promotes acute precision and rigidity, and can stifle creativity, flexibility, and imagination. People who live in mobile homes should minimize the addition of metal to their homes. Since Earth nourishes Metal, it would be well to minimize that element as well. Instead, go to the Controlling Cycle and let some Fire energetically "melt" the Metal. You can be plentiful with components of the Fire Element such as lighting, candles, shades of red and burgundy in decorating.

The Reduction Cycle will also help mitigate the metal. Use the Water Element to "dissolve" some of the Metal (such as a fountain – the larger the better). The goal is to maintain a balance of all Five Elements for optimum energetic harmony and comfort. Planting substantial trees and exterior foliage that give off negative ions will also help.

Practice Doing Your Elemental *Home*work

It is easy to practice doing an Elemental Assessment. Any time you find yourself waiting in a restaurant or doctor's reception area, or find yourself in any space with a few extra minutes, begin to look around and do an "Elemental count." Ask yourself which Elements are present and which are missing? Which ones are overly abundant and which are barely represented? Remember to consider the Elemental shapes as well as colors and the Elements themselves.

Soon you will become readily able to check out the Elemental scene and understand why you feel uneasy and uptight or happy and relaxed in any environment. This design philosophy of using the Five Elements is powerful and most interior designers practice it instinctively. They may not use this particular term, but they know which elements are lacking and what needs to be amplified with their decorating.

I encourage you to devote extra time to understanding, working with, and applying the Five Element Theory to property you are considering. This is one of the primary ways feng shui will serve you and give you handsome rewards as your rooms and landscaping resound with the balancing beauty of the Five Elements.

As you progress in your knowledge of feng shui, you will see that there are many layers to understand both in learning and application. The Elements are also associated energetically with the Life Aspirations of the bagua. For example, when wanting to increase the chi in the Wealth area, add more Wood and nourish it with Water. As you can see, feng shui is much more than moving furniture and hanging a crystal!

For a great selection of art designed for feng shui remedies and enhancements, visit Caroline Patrick's website at http://www. moongateschool.com/fengshui.html. Here you will find a large selection of beautiful art that has been designed from the Five Elements perspective to enhance your environment. (Caroline has made the site easy to use so you can click on any sector of the bagua to see art designed specifically to enhance that Life Area.)

Chapter 5 — Check Your *Chi* List

Do an Elemental evaluation of the lot or parcel.

__ Are all the Elements represented on the land? (+)

__ If you purchase this property will you be able to add Elemental adjustments to bring the land into balance? (+)

Check the Elements of the structure.

__ Are all the Elements represented within the dwelling? (+)

__ Does the flooring represent the Earth, Metal, or Wood Element? (+)

__ A mobile home is wrapped in metal. If you are considering a mobile home are you able to surround the home with substantial trees or foliage, especially red in color? (+)

__ A water feature such as a fountain is an excellent reducer for metal. Will you be able to add a fountain? (+)

Section II

Feng Shui Secrets for Land & Homes

Your Smartest Move — The Feng Shui Property Appraisal™

Ilona and Richard are exhausted. After several months of looking at houses they still have not found one that they both like. Ilona is a real estate investor and Richard is a retired college political science professor; they have many friends and entertain a lot.

Being "in the business," Ilona is very selective. They must have a one-level house, small, with an open floor plan for entertaining. Because of poor health and to avoid immune system problems, the home must have as many natural features as possible. Since many new floor coverings, finishes, and paint give off synthetic fumes which can trigger health problems, their search is doubly challenging.

They have found a great real estate agent, Robert, who understands their needs and is diligent in his search for new listings. To add to his professional strengths, Robert is a student of feng shui and understands many of the nuances that are critical to helping buyers select property using the guidelines of this age-old design science.

Several new listings came on the market over the weekend, and Robert spent time previewing them. There are two he wants Ilona and Richard to see right away. Some of the houses he rejected were located on either a "T" junction street or sat below grade. Another had a good floor plan, but the sloping driveway was a killer. He knows that showing those listings would be a waste of time. Their appointment is for Sunday mid-morning and both properties Robert has selected have reasonably good feng shui.

At the first house, Richard comments that the front entry and living area are exceptionally appealing; Ilona likes the kitchen with the sunny breakfast area. Robert mentions that despite all the good points, there is a missing corner in the Wealth Area. This can be corrected with some creative applications to the landscaping. The master bathroom has been remodeled and Richard can sense the synthetic materials used. The remodel looks great, but would be hard on his immune system. Otherwise the house feels good, is light and open; both Richard and Ilona like it.

The second property sits midway up a hill and has a great view. The gardens in the rear are inviting and Ilona and Richard enjoy being outdoors whenever possible. The house has not been remodeled which will allow them to use the natural renovation materials they require. The floor plan has the master bedroom in the right rear, southwest corner which is ideal. The office puts Richard facing his second Best Direction. Ilona and Richard can cook while facing the kitchen door, and the floor plan is ideal for entertaining.

Without hesitation, Ilona and Richard agree that the second house is close to their ideal. They are delighted that Robert has already seen it with "feng shui" eyes and saved them a lot of time filtering out houses with feng shui problems. "This is it!" they tell Robert. "Let's write it up!"

It Is Your Money

In a perfect world, when applying feng shui principles to real estate to achieve maximum results, you should first choose a plot of land that meets as many beneficial feng shui criteria as possible. Then you would design your home for that parcel according to your personal Positive Directions (found in the Special Supplement) and Eight Life Aspirations of the bagua. (Refer to Chapter 2.)

However, most of the time, a "perfect world" is not the world we get to deal with. Due to lack of time, money, building regulations, red tape, etc., the majority of real estate buyers purchase an existing house on a site chosen by an architect or developer. Usually, feng shui guidelines are never given a thought. Buyers then have to use feng shui enhancements and solutions to fix what was neglected, overlooked, or just done willy-nilly long ago.

That was then; this is now. We have the methods and skills to assess homes and land with better knowledge, *and* our feng shui eyes. Just remember, it is your money, so do not be like those who spend in haste and repent at leisure. A bit of extra time devoted now to important design issues will pay you handsome dividends later — both as you are living in this new house, and then in the future when you are the seller.

Buyers are telling their agents:
"Show me property that has good feng shui!"

A Few Assumptions Before We Begin

Let us agree you have decided to buy a house or property either for your personal residence or for an investment. Let's also assume you have already decided where you would like to live or invest.

The next assumption is that you have a basic idea of the size parcel and the number of bedrooms and bathrooms you will require. Hopefully you have given some thought to the square footage you would like.

104

Every buyer's house "wish" list is slightly different and unique. As you make your list of needs and wants, consider the importance of:

- ❑ a house with a view
- ❑ a formal dining space
- ❑ a room for an office
- ❑ an inside laundry
- ❑ a gourmet kitchen
- ❑ garage size

Other possibilities might be:

- ❑ a fireplace
- ❑ a tub in the master bath
- ❑ single-level or a home with stairs
- ❑ a fixer-upper (Are you the handy type?)
- ❑ a condominium with low maintenance and close neighbors
- ❑ privacy and a quiet setting

These are only a few considerations to ask yourself, but you get the idea. These are questions your real estate professional should also be asking you. A fireplace in the living room and a tub in the master bath are at the top of my list!

If you have not already created your "must" list and put your wants and needs in priority order, now is the time to do it. Take a few minutes and start to make your list at the back of this book. (I would suggest making this in pencil, for it will evolve as your search narrows.) Once your priorities are listed, number them in their order of importance.

Please spend quality time on this exercise. The purpose is to help you get clear about what you want in your next home or investment. Ask yourself what is *really* important for you to have in your next home. This list will become the foundation for your search (your time) and your spending (your money).

Avoid Buyers' Remorse — Do a Feng Shui Property Appraisal™

From an energetic and feng shui standpoint, if the feng shui of a place is all wrong, you cannot afford to be swept off your feet by a house that "charms" you or can be purchased for a "song." If the feng shui of the place is out of whack, even if you are willing to enclose the rear porch or add an extra bath, this is the perfect set-up for buyer's remorse.

Harry is the perfect example of feng shui buyer's remorse. After finalizing a difficult divorce, Harry bought a home in a hurry without giving serious thought to the neighborhood, the street he would be living on, or to the floor plan. The house seemed like a good buy at the time; it was in need of some deferred maintenance that he thought would be good to keep him busy — and the seller came down to his offered price.

Later Harry had a close friend from work who practiced feng shui for many years analyze the floor plan. His friend pointed out there was a missing Relationships area and there was a bathroom in the center of the home. High power lines close by towered over his property. The house sat very close to the street and the master bedroom was in the front of the house, just off the entry.

Several years after his purchase, Harry was suffering from severe depression and had lost his job. He admitted he never liked the house and had purchased it in an effort to get on with his life after the break-up of his marriage. He knew had made a big mistake.

The last thing you want after you have gone to all the trouble and expense of purchasing a piece of property, is to find out (now that the rose colored glasses are off) there are serious, irreversible defects that you wish you could change. To prevent these regrets there is an easy way to *"energetically" size up a property* and keep you focused on your priorities *and* good feng shui. I call it the *Feng Shui Property Appraisal*tm. Taking the time to do this assessment is the smartest move you can make.

In the course of your house-hunting you may see between 15 and 25 homes, sometimes more. You may really like only two or three. That is where the *Feng Shui Property Appraisal*™ comes in. Using feng shui to analyze a property is a simple exercise, and with practice should take you about 15 minutes. Time well spent! You will need to assemble a simple kit to take with you when you preview houses.

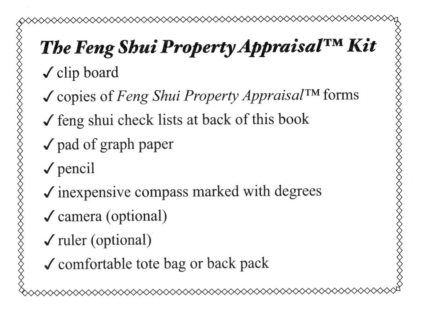

The Feng Shui Property Appraisal™ Kit

✓ clip board

✓ copies of *Feng Shui Property Appraisal™* forms

✓ feng shui check lists at back of this book

✓ pad of graph paper

✓ pencil

✓ inexpensive compass marked with degrees

✓ camera (optional)

✓ ruler (optional)

✓ comfortable tote bag or back pack

Doing this Feng Shui Property Appraisal is an important step. Try not to leave home without your kit — keep it handy and ready to go. When your agent calls to show you a great new listing in 15 minutes, you will be all set.

The Feng Shui Property Appraisal Kit

The Feng Shui Property Appraisal™

Make copies of this form from the tear-out section at the back of this book. First, fill out the preliminary information for each property: the address, date shown, agent, etc. Then, for each property you are considering:

Step 1— *Draw a simple floor plan.*

This drawing can be done on site at the kitchen or dining table after you have walked through the house completely. Use the space on the Appraisal form, or if you want to draw the plan on a larger scale, use the graph paper you have brought in your kit. If you would like, ask your agent to help you sketch a floor plan.

✓ Make your drawings in pencil and keep them simple, yet as proportionally accurate as possible. A ruler will help.

✓ Draw where all doors are located, including sliders or French doors.

✓ Show and label room locations, especially the master bedroom, kitchen, bathrooms, and laundry room.

Note: If the house has two stories, focus only on the main level for this exercise.

Sample floor plan… draw your own using extra paper if necessary.

Step 2 — *Fill out the Feng Shui Property Appraisal Checklist.*

This section at the back of this book is designed so you can remove the pages and make photocopies for each house you are considering.

✓ Fill out the checklist and be as objective as possible.

Step 3 — *Take a compass reading.*

✓ Holding your compass flat in your hand, at the front porch with your back to the front door, allow the needle to come to rest on the North reading. Adjust the "bevel" (the outside movable ring) so that the "N" lines up with the red end of the arrow. Note the *number of degrees* on the compass that the house is "facing." (For example: 30 degrees) Do not stand close to metal doors or metal gates as this can alter the reading. If you are uncertain as to which side of the house should be considered the "facing" side, remember the facing side is the side with the "strongest chi flow" (usually the side closest to the street).

✓ Write the direction (N, NE, W, SW, etc.) and the degree reading in the space provided.

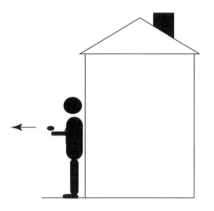

Take a compass reading with your back flat against the front door.

Hint: A compass is divided into 360 degrees. Magnetic North is zero degrees, East is 90 degrees, South is 180 degrees, West is 270 degrees. Any direction in between will fall within these quadrant degree numbers. Be as accurate as you can in determining your "facing" direction. This step is quite simple and should take just a few minutes.

Note: As you look at the street, if your front door is *not facing the same direction as the front wall of the house closest to the street,* take the compass reading with your back against the front wall not the front door.

Find the compass degree for the direction your house faces.

As you get serious about a property, it is helpful to also take a compass reading of the direction in which you think you will sleep (the direction the top of *your head will point* when you are lying down).

Step 4 — *Determine Your Positive Personal Directions*.

✓ Go to the Special Supplement page and determine your Positive Personal Directions.

Once you have done this, you will use the same Personal Direction information for each house.

Step 5 — *Assess your feelings.*

✓ Remind yourself at different times during a showing to take a "reading" of your feelings while at the property and especially inside the house. For example, if you feel uneasy or uncomfortable your score will be low (1 or 2). If you feel relaxed and happy in that space your score will be high (8 or 9).

✓ Score your overall feelings for this house on a scale of 1-10 (10 being best). Mark this score at the top of your sheet.

Note: If you have brought a camera, ask the agent or the owner for permission to photograph parts of the house you will especially want to remember. Most sellers will not mind, and these pictures may help make your final decision. It is both courteous and professional to get permission before taking photos.

Feng Shui Property Appraisal™

My feelings score: 7

Property Address: **915 SW TAYLOR**

Listing Office: **REALTY CO.**

Shown to me by: (agent or owner) **AGENT-RANDY FRIED**

Date of showing: **7/20** Approx. time of day: **6:15 PM**

Drawing of floor plan:

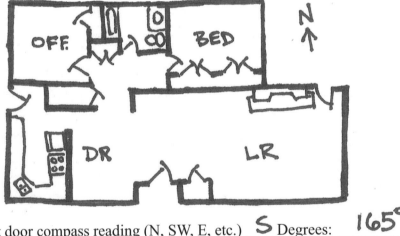

Front door compass reading (N, SW, E, etc.) **S** Degrees: **165°**

My 4 Positive Personal Directions are: **W, NE, SW, NW**

When sleeping, my bed will command the door: (**Yes** or No)

The direction my head will point when sleeping: **EAST**

When cooking, I will command the door: (Yes or **No**)

The direction I will face when cooking: **EAST**

Seated at my desk, I will command the door: (**Yes** or No)

The direction I will face when seated at my desk: **EAST**

Your final *Feng Shui Property Appraisal*™ will consist of::

❏ your completed Appraisal form

❏ your floor plan (either on the form or a separate paper)

❏ your completed copy of the *Check Your Chi List* from back of the book

❏ any photos you have taken

❏ real estate flyers, brochures, etc.

In order to preview houses in an organized way, it helps to keep all information about a particular property together (such as real estate flyers, photos, business card of agent who showed you the house, etc.). *Be systematic and organized — keep only information about houses that really interest you.*

After looking at four or five houses, you will forget the details. That is why it helps to take good notes or photos of your favorites; otherwise you will drown in confusion and still not remember things. Find an organizing system you like and stick with it.

By filing your *Feng Shui Property Appraisal*™ with the other information about each home you are seriously considering, you will quickly see a pattern emerging. You will feel more confident, focused, and certain of your feelings. When the best property (both energetically and one that meets your criteria) comes along, you will be ready to make an offer — for all the *right* reasons!

Your Agent Can Help

Take your real estate agent into your confidence and explain that you are using feng shui guidelines to assess the properties the agent will be showing you. You might be surprised at how eager your agent is to help and learn more about feng shui!

☯ Tip!

For your first viewing and best impression of a home, be sure you enter through the front main door. If the lock box is on a side door, have your agent come around and let you in through the main door. You want to enter the structure the way good energy will — through the "mouth of chi." Remember the main door is the primary entrance the architect designed for that purpose.

Seeing with Your New *"Feng Shui Eyes"*

As soon as you fine-tune the skill of trusting your intuition about a property, and following the feng shui suggestions in this book, you will be using your newly discovered "feng shui eyes." You will be able to look at four or five properties in a single session and, with practice, be able to skillfully assess how each house, neighborhood, and parcel measure up to your feng shui yardstick.

Chapter 6 — Check Your *Chi* List

These questions will help you practice *tap into your feelings* as you go about selecting a house to purchase. When you find yourself getting serious about a particular property, take time to go through this feng shui "smart moves" exercise:

___ On the drive to the house, do you inwardly smile as you approach the street? (+)

___ Do you have to go through "rough territory" in order to reach your prospective house? (-)

___ Is the surrounding neighborhood pleasant? (+)

___ Would you drive home from work one way more than another because that route makes you feel better? (+)

___ As you get closer to the house, do the nearby homes give you a feeling of pride (+) or disappointment? (-)

___ Do the adjacent homes on either side and directly in front of you give you a feeling of delight (+) or frustration? (-)

___ As you walk up the front path from the car, do you begin to feel yourself getting eager to see inside? (+)

Location, Location...
Feng Shui!

Patty and Ruel are actively looking for a new home. They want a well-built house with a yard for their two children, yet do not want to be slaves to a garden. The floor plan needs to facilitate supervising their young ones, yet give them plenty of privacy too.

Patty scouts new listings during the week, then she and Ruel go out together on the weekends leaving the kids with grandma. A quiet neighborhood with children in the area is a priority.

Mature trees in the neighborhood are important; they would rather have an older home with lots of surrounding trees than a newer neighborhood with brand new, skimpy plantings.

On Wednesday morning Patty found a great house with the right floor plan on a street with little traffic, mature trees lining the sidewalks, and a good school within walking distance. She is excited about bringing Ruel to see this one on Saturday.

Arriving mid-morning to view the property, Ruel notices the street is lined with cars, and they can hear music from a practicing band at the end of the block. A barking dog protecting the fence line noisily barks at them from next door. Although the canopy of trees is lovely, they wonder if the house will make up for the excess traffic, rock music, and barking dog.

The owner is welcoming and their agent points out the benefits of the easy-care back yard and open, near-perfect floor plan. They stay long enough to hear the band finish its second set, thank the owner, and flee, asking their agent to focus on what a property would be like all week, not just on quiet weekdays. They are back to square one.

How to Really Check Out the Neighborhood

Too many times I have shown an attractive property on a quiet Wednesday afternoon only to come back the following Saturday and see an entirely different picture. Weekdays, the streets are usually empty with only a few parked cars; the neighborhood is so quiet you can hear the leaves rustling on the trees. But visit the same street on a weekend, and chances are you cannot find a parking place, driveways and streets are jammed with cars, and a local rock group is practicing in full swing.

> ## ☯ Tip!
>
> Visit a property you are serious about on different days and at different times. Get to know the personality of the neighborhood on weekends as well as weekdays.

Your new neighborhood and community at large are macro systems of energy that will impact your new street and home. So take the time to familiarize yourself with the chi of the area to discover the fascinating shops, cafes, library, mall, etc. that make up the heart and soul of your new larger neighborhood. This chapter will focus on feng shui issues in the general vicinity of your potential new home. The next chapter will help you evaluate the micro energetic implications of the street where you might live.

Another Chance to Do your *Home*work

Your real estate professional has general information about the community, but *you* must do the follow-up with some detective work. Before you make an offer on a home, find out from the city or county planning department if any proposed changes in the area will adversely affect your property.

A big part of buyer's remorse is finding out *after* close of escrow that the local train whistles through at three in the morning or that a new freeway has just been approved two blocks away. Keep in mind I have been a real estate broker for nearly three decades; this advice has more to do with real estate savvy than feng shui, but I want you to enjoy your new home on every level!

Nice surprises are great; the other kind are just surprises and are most often unpleasant. Of course, your real estate agent should know about most anything that is on the drawing boards that would adversely affect your property or peace of mind and inform you accordingly; but be sure to do your own sleuthing. A new house is too big an investment not to be fully informed. "Why didn't I check it out?" should not be your post-purchase mantra, a constant reminder of a poor feng shui/real estate decision.

Are You *Scrunched* by Taller Houses on Either Side?

Don't feel dwarfed! Feng shui awareness includes the energy of surrounding properties, especially your neighbors directly adjacent to your house. *Are any of these dwellings significantly taller than the home you are considering*? If so, at the very least, you will need to plant fast growing trees on your property between you and the higher neighbor. The trees are not to spoil neighbors' views, but rather to *protect your* energy and privacy.

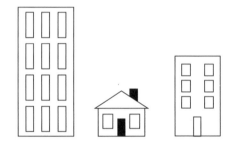

Oppressing Chi from Higher Surrounding Buildings

It is unnerving to go out your back door or open a bedroom window and know your neighbor has a direct line of sight into your private world. Taller structures around us invade our space visually and it can be a difficult, if not impossible, condition to correct.

Chi from taller buildings that surround homes or offices tends to "push down" on our chi, making us feel energetically smaller, less significant, and less confidant. This is especially true when the higher building is massive and pretentious. There are feng shui solutions to block prying views. However, if you avoid this problem in the first place, you will be far better off. If you are absolutely head-over-heels in love with a smaller dwelling nestled among tall towers, get thee to a good nursery and start planting those privacy-protecting trees!

Churches or Graveyards Nearby?

Feng shui considers the large interior spaces of churches, temples, and synagogues to be sources of highly concentrated *yin* energy. Though uplifting services and celebrations such as weddings take place in churches, they are also often used for funerals and memorial services.

Graveyards are the epitome of yin energy and feng shui principles guide you to avoid having your home (which is filled with life and benevolent chi) positioned close to resting places for the dead. Furthermore, as land becomes scarce, housing developments may be built over ancient burial sites that were often located in sacred places with spectacular views.

Following feng shui guidelines we are advised to treat these sites with respect, and to leave them undisturbed. When we try and build over sacred ground, we are provoking serious feng shui consequences, and homes built on burial sites are not energetically comfortable. *Yang living is not compatible with yin resting. (The living do not sleep with the dead.)* The two places need to be separated from one another by walls, natural foliage, or topography such as gentle hills.

The same applies to sites near hospitals, mortuaries, crematoriums, or slaughterhouses. As places of suffering and death, these would be highly inauspicious locations. For yang living locations, from a predecessor energy point of view (explained more fully in Chapter 10), *avoid sites where these types of buildings were ever located.* The residual yin chi is so overpowering that it would be similar to building a home over a graveyard. Discovering this earlier land usage is challenging, yet do-able.

If your instincts tell you your potential property is a prime candidate for such a site, the best place to begin your research is City Hall records or the local historical society.

Other sites to avoid living near are landfills, waste disposal sites, and hazardous materials dumping areas. Much evidence shows that houses built near toxic dumps cause serious health problems for residents. No view or bargain is worth jeopardizing a family's health. Do not even think about it. Often land is reclaimed, meaning it was previously a wetland habitat and has now been covered over and filled with soil allowing it to be built upon. Be very cautious with filled in wetlands; remember water will have its own way eventually. I would advise against purchasing property built on a previous wetland site.

All the above considerations are part of the "natal energy" of a property referred to in Chapter 1. Natal energy is extremely important and is like the energetic package that a property is "born" with. Positive natal energy is beneficial and usually brings owners years of enjoyment. Conversely, negative natal energy that cannot be changed or reversed proves to be a constant source of buyer's remorse.

Where's the Shade?

"A civilization flourishes when people plant trees under whose shade they will never sit."

— *Greek Proverb*

Here is a feng shui secret: When looking for your new castle, be it modest or magnificent in price and glory, have it sheltered from the elements by as many natural aces in your hand as possible. Among other things we will discuss, this means trees, foliage, and rolling hills. With the bounty of nature on your side, you are on the way to finding a property with excellent feng shui.

When I started studying feng shui, the importance of trees around properties became clear to me. Besides being beautiful, trees raise the chi! Healthy trees are so loaded with good chi that they replenish our spirits as well as our bodies with shade and cool, moist yin energy; tree energy counter-balances the expansive yang stressful energy of most environments.

Trees are easy and fun to plant; they help cleanse the air by giving off negative ions (the good ones!) and they also help reduce global warming. Trees provide habitats for birds and animals, and they add beauty to our world in quantum amounts. The leaves provide humus to enrich the soil and exercise for us to get outdoors in the fall to do the raking. Another big bonus, according to the National Arbor Day Foundation, "Trees around your home can increase its value by 15% or more!" (www.arborday.org)

In the past few decades and still today, new housing developments have sprung up wherever builders can buy land close to existing cities. Mature trees are often sacrificed to maximize a profit from the costly land. Sadly, trees often get in the way of a developer's plans.

But wiser builders pay for the planting of mature trees among their just-built houses. Whether they know it is good feng shui or not, they do it. Somehow they sense the value of trees and know the expense of planting them results in faster and more profitable sales. They are right.

Here's Pointing at You, Kid

Beside the positive aspects of natural elements such as hills, trees, and foliage affecting your potential property, some man-made structures have negative energetic effects on real estate. (Remember those pointy rooflines from neighboring houses that send negative sha energy your way?)

Water towers and storage tanks that loom above residential neighborhoods energetically overwhelm the houses they are closest to and visually affect the entire area they serve. *Avoid buying your home where a water tower dominates the landscape or is close to your property.* Water towers and large storage tanks can be unstable in earthquakes or other natural disasters such as hurricanes and cyclones. Being in their path should they topple or break loose is not good common sense or good feng shui.

Water storage tank towers over condominiums.

The large *satellite dish* is another common man-made feature to be energetically aware of, especially the older variety, still prevalent in some areas, that points its huge dish shape toward neighboring homes. This situation constitutes a sha poison arrow and should be avoided.

Most of the older satellite dishes are being replaced with the newer 18-inch diameter models; however, if you absolutely fall in love with a home that is near a large satellite dish pointing your way, you can plant some fast growing trees that will block out your view of the dish. Placing a mirror outside, facing the dish will transcendentally send the negative chi back and away from you (refer to Appendix C). Energetically, that is about the best you can do.

Large satellite dishes still exist and are sources of sha chi.

Large antennae for televisions or ham radios, perching upon neighboring roofs and (like antennae of any kind) are poison arrows that send continual sha chi toward nearby dwellings. Again, the solution is to visually block the antennae by planting trees, or on a smaller scale, hanging a crystal, or a plant in the closest window so that you do not have to constantly look at the visually offensive culprit.

Antennae and large satellite dishes do not need to be deal breakers, but avoiding them is still best. You want the most beneficial natal energy for your home possible. Many details contribute to the final energetic picture for your new location, so take them all into consideration and sift through the ones that have the most negative impact. Too many negatives will certainly tip the scales and motivate you to look elsewhere.

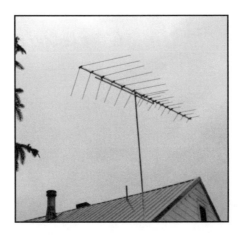

Large roof antenna aimed your way is a sha arrow.

Do not hesitate to share with your real estate agent all these ideas that are becoming important to you. Let your agent in on your feng shui secrets and they will be better able to fine-tune your home search. Real estate agents' time is valuable too and they want to find the house that pleases you sooner rather than later.

Chapter 7 — Check Your *Chi* List

__ Are there homes or buildings near you that make you feel energetically overwhelmed? (-)

__ Are there churches, temples, synagogues, graveyards, hospitals, or mortuaries in the vicinity? (-)

__ Is the home you are considering built over a previous wetland? (-)

__ It takes a long time to grow a majestic tree. Any property with mature, healthy landscaping gets bonus feng shui points. (+)

__ Is there energetic support such as a hill or trees behind and to the sides of the property? (+)

__ Is there a water tower, or large water storage tank nearby? (-)

__ Are there any satellite dishes or large roof antennae pointing your way? (-)

8

Streets, Lot Shapes, and Your Lucky Numbers

Marie and Ben are looking for a retirement hideaway. They both value privacy and put a high priority on a quality neighborhood. They will live on their boat a good portion of the year, so it is important that security and helpful neighbors are in place to keep an eye on things when they are away.

Ben and Marie want a home for quiet entertaining and a studio for her to paint in. An ocean view is a high priority and they would sacrifice interior space for a great view. Ben is very handy and a good garage workspace is important to him.

Over several months, their agent, Henry, has previewed many houses for them. He found a condominium complex that sits high on a hill overlooking the ocean. Two condos are available in the same complex — one sits forward in the development and juts out from the rest; the second sits further back and is more sheltered. Both have a third bedroom with good light for Marie's studio, and the entertaining area is satisfactory in each.

Looking first at the condo with the floor plan that juts out, they think that view will be the best. As Marie eagerly steps out onto the balcony, the wind grabs her newspaper and lifts it high over her head. Watching it swirl down to the ground below, Ben looks at Marie with his mind already made up. He loves to read and relax outside with his newspaper and books — this windy perch will never do.

In the condo that is tucked farther back into the complex, they wonder how that balcony will feel. The view is not quite as spectacular, yet they can sit easily in the sheltered area because it is out of the wind. Ben feels more comfortable here and the position of this unit will allow them to keep the French doors to the balcony open most of the day.

Ben smiles at Marie and then says to Henry, "Let's go back to the office and make an offer."

Siting for Success

Location is much more than just the street where you live and the parcel you buy. Location is made up of many things: your town or city, the overall neighborhood, the roads entering your immediate neighborhood, the specific street, and the houses around your parcel. Remember, *the site is far more important than the house.* Do not be taken in by cosmetic touches to a structure. Superficial fixes will not make up for a blighted neighborhood or an unpleasant approach to your castle.

If you do succumb to poor judgment and purchase in a questionable location, you will have plenty of time to think about your error. You may even have to take a financial loss just to get out of the neighborhood. Nothing is more important than buying in a good location.

The High Price for Living a "High Life"

One of the harshest aspects nature can hurl at us is wind and in feng shui, the "feng" translates directly as "wind." Gentle breezes are the feng shui ideal, so check out the weather, especially how the prevailing winds affect your potential dwelling. Having a super view is wonderful; but if you live at the top, or very close to the summit of a hill, the days that you enjoy the outdoors will be limited.

Feng shui is all about balance and living in harmony with the natural environment. When the wind comes too harshly it disturbs our inner chi; it makes us feel uncomfortable and we are driven indoors, unable to enjoy the outside beauty. In feng shui, the top of a hill or mountain is referred to as the "head of the dragon" and as such is an energetically precarious house location.

If a view site is a priority, be prepared to compromise a bit; the best feng shui position is about one-third of the way down from the top of a hill (refer to the feng shui armchair position explained in Chapters 1 and 4). This location still gives you a wonderful view, and the protection of the hill in the rear will prevent you from being buffeted by strong winds. You will smile as you step outside, sheltered from the winds found on hilltops. As I am sure you have noticed, much of feng shui is really ordinary common sense.

Get Street Smart

Your street has huge feng shui (and real estate) significance, and you will not want to proceed further until you know the importance of various shapes, formations, and types of streets. This chapter will show you the energetic implications of different streets and how benevolent chi is affected by each of these types.

As explained earlier, in ancient China, rivers and dirt pathways were the streets. Only later did roads, avenues, cul-de-sacs, and highways become important when choosing a home site. Today we have freeways, truck routes, bus lines, and train tracks to mention a few of the road hazards to contend with. Because of the stressful chi of today's world with its frenetic highways, it helps to have some guidelines about various types of roads in order to improve your odds of buying a feng shui beneficial property.

Experienced real estate agents learn early in their careers that when driving clients to houses, they should take the nicest route possible and try to avoid whatever might be unsightly along the way. You may be driving to your new home several times a day, so make sure your "way home" is one that does not depress you.

The actual journey to your home may seem like a small consideration, but the closer you get to your sacred space, the more you should see attractive neighborhoods and dwellings. The feng shui goal here is that the nearer you get to your personal castle, you should happily anticipate your arrival on an inner, energetic level. Pleasant sights along the route will allow you to look forward to your return from work each day.

T and Y Junctions —
Dirty Work at the Crossroads

A T-junction is just what it sounds like — a road that is joined or intersected by another road at a 90 degree angle, making a perpendicular (or near perpendicular) junction. Houses that sit at or near this T intersection receive an extraordinary amount of sha cutting chi from the cars and headlights continually aiming straight towards them and the all-important mouth of chi. Depending on the amount of traffic, this condition is a source of high energetic stress and anxiety.

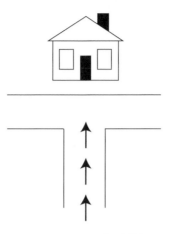

A house at a T-junction receives the full brunt of sha energy.

A close cousin to the T-junction is a Y-junction site. Homes and businesses positioned at or near the crook or neck of roads forming a Y shape also receive huge doses of negative sha chi from cars and headlights constantly aimed their way. This serious feng shui challenge creates a ceaseless, water torture effect. A home purchased in this type of location will be difficult to live in and will be hard to sell when you finally cannot take it any longer.

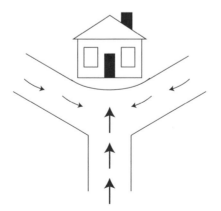

Properties located at a Y junction receive large doses of cutting sha chi.

A few feng shui solutions are available to make it marginally possible to live at a T or a Y junction site, such as planting large trees, substantial hedges, or building protective walls across the front property line. However you try to solve this feng shui problem, living in this setting will always deplete your chi and all your attempts to create good chi will be a constant up-hill battle.

Again, this is why you are reading this book! Far better to avoid a seriously negative feng shui condition than have to correct it after a purchase. I strongly suggest you pass over houses sited in this way, and do not let yourself be talked into purchasing for any other seemingly good reason. Just go on to the next selection.

Enjoy the Space that Separates You from the Street

The feng shui ideal is to have the dwelling located within the center one-third of the property. Give your prospective house extra bonus chi points if:

    ☯ there is an especially deep front yard

- the property has a circular driveway

- the house sits on a slight rise

All of these spatial factors allow the benevolent chi to approach your house slowly and abundantly. If your property is anywhere near a major highway that emanates stressful sha chi, this large front distance from the road is especially important — it acts like an energetic buffer zone.

Remember these tips are suggestions, yet definitely worth considering as you are hot in pursuit of your ideal feng shui house. Try to stay as far away as possible from the energy of freeways, busy streets, bus routes, train tracks, and commercial districts.

The Driveway: A Skateboard Ramp Is *Not* What You Want

Akin to roads, yet even closer to home, is your driveway. Driveways, and any problems they may have, belong *completely* to you, the homeowner.

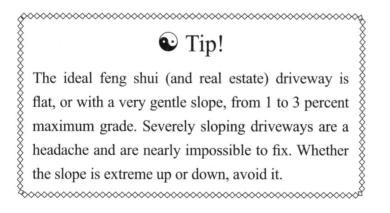

☯ Tip!

The ideal feng shui (and real estate) driveway is flat, or with a very gentle slope, from 1 to 3 percent maximum grade. Severely sloping driveways are a headache and are nearly impossible to fix. Whether the slope is extreme up or down, avoid it.

Good builders know that if they have to build on a sloping lot, one of the most difficult design concessions they and future owners will have to deal with is the driveway slope. Construction workers detest a challenging road incline: a steep driveway is hard on vehicles, especially the brakes. Off-loading building materials (and later people and groceries) will always be difficult.

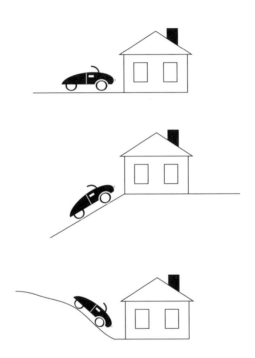

Flat driveways are ideal. Sloping ones will drive you crazy.

Severely down-sloping driveways present the additional problem of inadequate water drainage away from the property, especially the garage. Down-sloping driveways are a red flag to real estate agents who have to fill out their own disclosure statements. Signs of moisture buildup, mold, mildew, or water stains of any kind are a tip-off to the problem of poor drainage. Correcting these water problems can be very expensive. Someday you will be a seller — do not get caught with this problem.

Know Your (Cul-de-Sac) Place

Homes located within a cul-de-sac or a "closed road" have their own set of chi challenges to contend with. As shown in the diagram below, houses at the apex or top bulb position of a cul-de-sac get the majority of the sha chi buffeting from traffic and headlights (referred to in feng shui as the "tiger's eyes").

Dwellings closest to the beginning of the cul-de-sac receive this distractive sha chi to a lesser degree depending on how far from the top bulb they are positioned. The houses located on either side toward the bottom of the bulb tend to receive the least difficult chi.

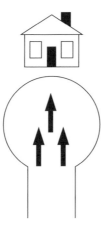

House at the top of a cul-de-sac receives the greatest amount of sha chi.

Curing this setting at the top of a cul-de-sac with protective trees, foliage, walls, or fences is an added burden to the buyer, so do not select this problem location in the first place.

139

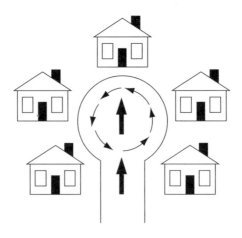

Houses on each side of a cul-de-sac receive far less sha chi. Note how the chi becomes trapped in a cul-de-sac.

A clear statement of where this road is going.

A close relative of the cul-de-sac is the "dead-end" street. Since feng shui is a language of metaphors it will not take you long to figure out that living on a dead-end street (which is usually clearly posted as such for the world to see) means you are symbolically going nowhere. At least on a cul-de-sac, the chi (like the automobiles) has a chance to circulate and get out.

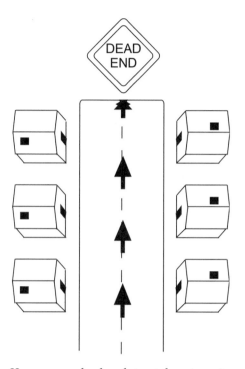

Houses on a dead-end street do not receive circulating, abundant chi.

Metaphorically speaking, a house situated at a dead-end is positioned where the chi is blocked and can go no further. Chi, like water, has no "reverse" gear — it does not go backwards or climb up hill from a lower position. *Good fortune and benevolent blessings do not go down dead-ends.*

On the other hand, dead-end streets are usually quiet and private. There is no through traffic and the only cars will be those of residents and guests. These streets can be protective of people who are going through a "healing" period in their lives — when being without a lot of chi from the outside world may be what they need in order to complete the healing process be it physical or emotional. Just be aware that dead-end streets will lack the abundant chi that most people find strengthening and beneficial.

Protect Your Rear Flank

Caesar and Attila the Hun were both correct: never leave your rear or flanks exposed and open to attack. Think like Caesar thought as you are house hunting, and look for a property that has some natural protection to the rear and sides of the lot. This protective element can be as simple as a row of trees, a high fence, a mountain, or hill.

Note: You do not want a hill immediately behind your house. Think about water run-off and the powerful yang energy of the mountain constantly bearing down on you. You want to provide support and shielding from weather and any negative sha chi (Refer to Chapter 2) that may come from behind or from either side.

In China, the harshest winds come from the North, and so temples, palaces, and homes of those who follow feng shui are built with their backs to the North. Ask yourself from which direction do the winds and the harshest weather come from in your area? Select a property with its rear and flanks protected.

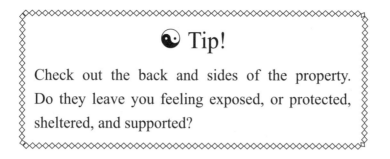

☯ Tip!

Check out the back and sides of the property. Do they leave you feeling exposed, or protected, sheltered, and supported?

Remember, once you have moved in, it is not easy to pick up and move if you are unhappy. Consider how you are energetically supported in your new house before signing on the dotted line. (For more explanation, review the "classic armchair position" in Chapter 4.)

Is Your Lot Shape a Feng Shui Bonanza?

You may not know it, but the house you are thinking of buying may be sitting on a lot shape that is a feng shui gold mine. After considering the community, neighborhood and street, next think about the shape of your lot. Some shapes are much more auspicious than others, and since much of feng shui is symbolic and made up of visual clues that have energetic implications, the parcel's shape is no exception.

In order to discover your potential lot shape you need a bird's eye view of the lot. This can be found on a set of house plans, on a parcel map, or a "plat map" and can usually be obtained through the city planning or building department. (A plat map is used by the county assessor's office for tax and identification purposes). Often the owner or your real estate agent can obtain one. This is an easy, yet important, feng shui step if you are getting close to making an offer.

Do Not Assume Anything

The physical configuration of your lot will most likely be a "regular" one, meaning a square or a rectangle, which is the feng shui ideal. However, parcels often have non-parallel sides, "doglegs," or they are narrow in the back, wide in the front, or vise versa. *Follow a basic real estate rule: do not ever assume anything.*

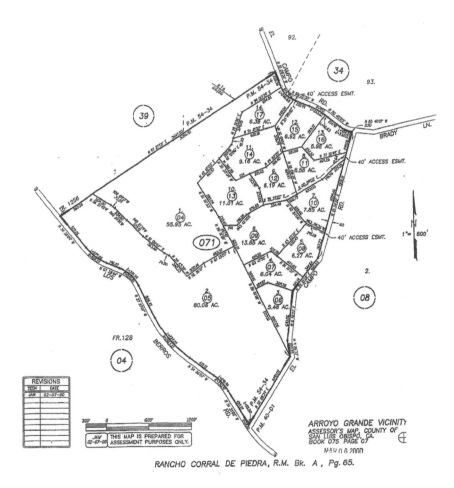

A Typical Plat Map

New buyers often think a back fence is their boundary line, until they find out after close of escrow, that the large drainage culvert behind the fence also belongs to them (and they have to maintain it!); or the rear neighbor built that fence years ago and still thinks the property line is five feet into your back yard.

A fence is just a fence. It does not necessarily indicate where properties are legally divided, and those who think fences are property lines are often sadly mistaken. This is why surveys locating boundary markers are so important!

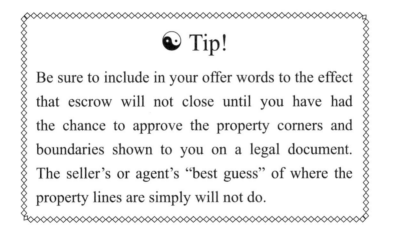

☯ Tip!

Be sure to include in your offer words to the effect that escrow will not close until you have had the chance to approve the property corners and boundaries shown to you on a legal document. The seller's or agent's "best guess" of where the property lines are simply will not do.

In feng shui (and real estate) we only want happy surprises. Do the following to avoid the unhappy ones:

- ✓ Obtain a parcel, or plat, map
- ✓ Locate all four (or more) corner markers of your potential property. If they are not easily discovered, make finding and approving them a condition of your offer. The cost of locating survey corners can be paid for by the seller, the buyer, or can be shared by both, including agents.

✓ Determine where *easements* are located for purposes of utility services, wells, ingress and egress of neighbors, etc. The title company and real estate agent can help you find out exactly where easements are.

Now you are ready to do some feng shui analysis of the shape of your potential parcel. Compare it to those shown below.

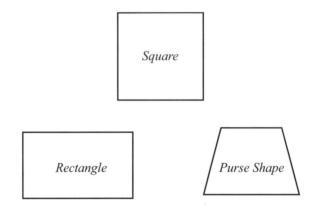

These regular lot shapes are considered auspicious feng shui selections.

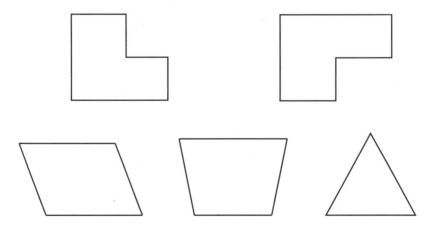

Irregular lots are not auspicious. Various life Aspiration areas will be missing when the bagua is laid over the entire parcel of land.

Getting down to Earth

Another important factor to consider is the quality of the soil of your new lot. This will be more critical to those who garden, but everyone should consider the soil. Good, rich earth is an excellent clue to good chi; parcels with dead or dying plants and withering natural vegetation is a tip-off that something is not quite right.

In earlier times, wise and successful farmers would smell and even taste the soil before buying a piece of land. Soil that smelled or tasted sour was considered out of the question. They knew that good crops require rich dirt, and that it is much easier to start with quality soil than to pay for expensive fertilizers and soil amendments.

Barren areas or patchy spots of particularly rocky or poor soil may indicate the land cannot support lush plant life and therefore could adversely affect the chi of the inhabitants. Expert gardeners know that if the land has no worms, the soil quality is probably poor. Of course, truckloads of amendments will help, but over time will deplete your bottom line. The land may be suffering from a serious case of neglect. Previous owners who have experienced misfortune or been absent from the property for long periods will often inadvertently contribute to poor soil conditions.

Take a Hint from Nature

Classical feng shui advises us to look for signs of healthy animal chi in and around property. (Dogs constantly barking or snapping next door do not qualify.) Birds nesting in trees, squirrels, and other naturally occurring wildlife are considered auspicious and good indicators that the chi of the land is bountiful.

If animals do not like to live there, what do they know that we don't? Dead birds or animals found at a particular site are considered ill feng shui omens and when viewing property, if you encounter dead animals, no matter how trivial or natural it may seem, be cautious. As always, check your own senses and your intuition. Do the parcel and surroundings give you a good feeling? If not, jump back in the car and zoom down the road.

Be Careful of Water *behind* You: Rivers, Streams, Creeks, and Pools

"Topography" refers to the features on the surface of land. Since feng shui is all about chi and how it moves in a particular space, features such as hills, large rocks, streams, and wooded areas have important energetic ramifications.

Mountains and hills are considered to be yang in nature, as are large rocks and boulder formations. Elements like these are usually best to the rear of a parcel as they give energetic support to a structure. Boulders in the front of a property can also act as energetic guardians and are auspicious as long as they do not block the chi trying to enter through the main door.

Waterways, however, are usually considered yin in nature and are definite feng shui assets when in the front of a property. Swimming pools, of course, are usually positioned in the rear yard for privacy and seclusion. A large body of water such as a swimming pool has significant yin energy and needs to be grounded with Earth Elements such as boulders, a concrete deck, benches, or statuary. Rounded corners or elliptic, kidney-shaped pools with rounded edges are preferred to those with 90 degree corners which send sha chi toward the dwelling.

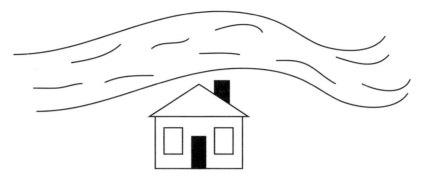

House with moving water to the rear allows
beneficial chi to exit quickly.

A fast moving river or creek behind a dwelling is considered troublesome from a feng shui standpoint because the water, symbolizing abundance, moves too quickly and takes the benevolent chi away before it can accumulate and benefit the property.

Traditionally, this condition symbolizes loss of wealth and a constant state of financial troubles. Sites along a river or creek need to have significant foliage, trees, or boulders in place along the banks to prevent erosion as well as to help prevent the good chi from leaving the parcel. *Many followers of feng shui would avoid a property with a swift creek or river directly at the rear of the lot.*

Street Names – Take Comfort in Their Strength

It may seem unusual to place significance in the name of a particular street. However, since feng shui places great emphasis on symbols and metaphors, it is important to consider the implications of street names, which, like everything else, have energy and send symbolic messages.

Would you rather live on Easy Street or Hurricane Hill? How about Rapid Lightening Way or Lakeview Drive? This is a rather minor consideration in the grand feng shui scheme of things, and other situations such as a T junction site or fast moving water (or road) behind a property carry greater energetic consequences. However, for feng shui purposes, consider the energetic significance of the name of your potential street, making sure it is one you want to be associated with for a long time.

The name of your street sends a subtle message.

These are very personal yet definite choices. You can live on Clinton Court or Reagan Drive, Mercedes Lane or Tumbleweed Terrace, the decision is yours. Remember, every time you put your return address on an envelope or give directions for friends, family, or clients to find your house, you energetically reinforce the symbolic significance of the name of your street.

You may find the perfect house, but if it sits on a street named Widow's Peak Way or Chicken Coop Road, go back to the basic feng shui rule and analyze how this makes you feel. In a way, just like your home, this street name is an energetic reflection of you. Remember, *you are your feng shui and your feng shui is you.*

Is Your Castle at the Bottom of a Well?

Now consider the "grade level" of your property in relation to the street. To be higher than street level is great. An elevated position is good feng shui because the energy reaches upward and circulates within your space.

However, a site lower than street level, like being at the bottom of a well, is not auspicious and should be avoided. The auspicious chi has to sink to find you and a position such as this will always be vulnerable to water run-off from heavy rains and vehicles running off the road squarely into your unprotected property.

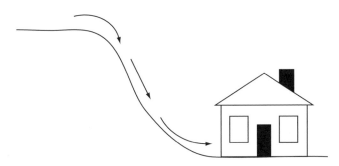

House below street level challenges chi to find you.

Houses below street level are energetically compromised and must always deal with an uphill struggle. There is really no solution — you just live with it. Anxiety, depression, lack of confidence, and constant worry is the energetic package that accompanies a property below street level. Savvy buyers will avoid properties with this condition. Be aware of a situation that you can never correct. Remember, someday you will be trying to sell this property.

One-way Streets Move Energy Quickly

Another caution for your feng shui site selection is the property located on a *one-way street*. Some communities have many one-way streets, others have few or none. On one-way streets, the chi moves in one direction only, and generally the chi is moving quickly. Properties benefit from more good chi on slow-moving, two-way streets.

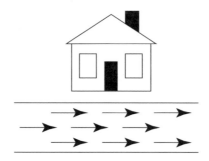

Chi moves quickly on a one-way street.

The chi that does come down a one-way street can move so rapidly it has no time to stop along the way and bring you abundant blessings. The chi moves especially fast on one-way streets with two or three lanes. Here the trick is to slow the chi down so that abundance and blessings do not pass you by.

Your Lucky Number — the Auspicious Address

The Chinese place great significance on numbers and their auspicious energies. Yes, house numbers are symbolic, and you might as well take house numbers into consideration if the energy of numbers is significant to you.

Most of us have what we would call "lucky numbers." How nice it would be if our numerical address added up to our lucky number, or we had one or more of that number at the front of our house every time we pulled into our driveway! The feng shui implications for numbers is in Appendix B if you are curious.

Often the energetic association has to do with the pronunciation of a particular number. The number 4 in Chinese is pronounced almost exactly like the word for death. In Chinese neighborhoods throughout the world you will find very few houses or businesses with the digit 4. Further, many Chinese hotels will avoid naming a floor the 4th floor, just as Western hotels often avoid naming the 13th floor. This is more of a cultural implication than a feng shui consideration, yet it can apply to some buyers, so it is mentioned here.

Some feng shui practitioners may advise having an address with one or two of the numbers relating to your birth date to indicate that you will live in the house for a long time.

An address with the number 8 is considered auspicious.

The number 8 is considered extremely auspicious, and I have had clients who will go out of their way to have an address with as many 8s as possible. "Eight" sounds like the word for "multiply" and represents good luck. It is considered to be a "fertile" number. If you desire many sons, live in a house with eight in the address.[4] In Hong Kong, telephone numbers and license plates with 8s are at a premium, and an address with 888 is a total feng shui bonanza. Lucky sellers with this address can add several thousand dollars to the asking price for this feature alone!

There Is No Perfect 10

Feng shui is about compromise and making choices. It is important to remember that very few perfect feng shui parcels or houses exist — most need remedies for one or more feng shui defects. Your challenge is to sift through the most important considerations, then select a property that has as many feng shui benefits as possible. The perfect 10 of feng shui property will probably elude you, but do not worry that you will have to live with a less than satisfactory new home. Determine where you need feng shui enhancements, and by using this book, you will know how best to go about doing just that. What I want you to have is the information that will guide you to the best possible energetic choice of new property that will serve you well for many years.

When analyzing property to purchase, whether it is an undeveloped lot, or an already built house, seriously consider all the feng shui tips in this chapter as they apply to the site on which you are going to spend so much money. Fine-tune your house hunting with your new feng shui

---

[4] *Feng Shui: How to Achieve the Most Harmonious Arrangement of Your Home and Office,* Angel Thompson. P.71.

eyes, and your search for real estate will take on a new and heightened dimension.

Some less than desirable things can be mitigated — trees can be planted, boulders can be placed, paint can be applied. However, once purchased, you cannot change the natal energy of where your house sits on the lot, the shape or the name of your street, or your address — you can only work with what you have. Making a wise choice should now be easier.

Chapter 8 — Check Your *Chi* List

__ Is your potential lot on or close to the top of a hill? (-)

__ Is the property you are looking at located on a T or Y intersection? (- -) If yes, keep looking.

__ Is there a major highway or heavily trafficked road close by? (-)

__ Is there a comfortable distance between the house and the street? (+)

__ Does the property have a steeply sloping driveway? (-)

__ Is it at the top of a cul-de-sac? (- -)

__ Is the property on a closed, dead-end street? (-)

__ Is the shape of your parcel a rectangle or square? (+)

__ Does the property have good, rich soil? (+)

__ Is there a fast moving creek, river, or road behind the property? (-)

__ Does the name of the street have pleasant or at least a neutral energetic association for you? (+)

__ Is the home above (+) or below (-) street level?

__ Is the house located on a one-way street? (-)

__ Do the house address numbers contain or add up to one of your lucky numbers? (+)

A Feng Shui Close-up
of Your Castle

Karin and Barton are not difficult buyers; they just know exactly what they want. They would rather wait and keep looking instead of settling for a home they may regret purchasing. They have been looking for over a year.

Both want a contemporary home; Karin has a great sense of style and Barton is the practical, handy sort who needs a good garage-workshop. Karin likes to entertain and also wants a very special master bedroom — a sanctuary away from the stress of their busy lives. She needs a functional and well-appointed kitchen next to an ample dining space; not a room off by itself, but an area for a large table with plenty of chairs. Karin also loves to garden and would enjoy a craft room.

Karin's friend who knows about feng shui warned her to avoid floor plans with a bathroom in the center of the house and stairs that face the front door. She also told Karin not to purchase a house on a T junction, or one that sits below grade level.

Barb, their experienced agent, is sharp and a hard worker. She has been combing the new listings for just the right home for Karin and Barton, yet even she is beginning to get discouraged. The market has changed since she started helping them, and now has fewer and fewer homes to choose from.

One weekend while they were out looking, Karin spotted a house in a great neighborhood where the FOR SALE sign was just being put up. The landscaping was delightful, and the lines of the home were stately, yet not too formal. The lawn was freshly trimmed and bedding plants lined the edges of the gently curved walkway. Barb immediately made an appointment for them to take a look.

At the front porch Barton commented on the oval lead-glass panel in the oak door. The brass porch light, door handle, and knob were sparkling. Fragrant blossoms of colorful flowers spilled over the sides of several planters and the sound of a fountain next to the porch was delightful as they waited for the owner to come to the door.

The interior was immaculate and in the entryway a beautiful bouquet of fresh flowers greeted them. Karin could immediately see the large dining area just past the family room and her eyes lit up. The kitchen was great. Barton was anxious to see the garage, so they went there next. These owners had done a wonderful job keeping the house in excellent condition. By this time there were smiles all around.

The master bedroom was smaller than they had

hoped, but the master bath with its large Jacuzzi tub made up for that. Their room was at the far right rear area of the house, and Karin's feng shui friend had told her this was considered lucky for a happy marriage.

They figured that the fourth bedroom could be a craft room for Karin, and as Barton went into the garage for another look, Karin went with him and they talked together. When they returned, they were both grinning. "This is it!" they both said, and asked Barb to go back to the office to write the offer.

Honey, Stop the Car!

As agents drive our clients by a particular property for sale, we love to hear them ask us to slow down — then they take a deep breath and say, "Wow!" When this happens, we are close to finding a site that has good energy and good feng shui. When real estate agents take a listing, we hope the property will already have great curb appeal. When a property has this quality, the hardest part of attracting a buyer is already taken care of. All sellers and listing agents want potential buyers to say, "Honey, stop the car!"

For better or for worse, first impressions for buyers happen fast. Properties that have great curb appeal speed up this process of a good first impression because the buyers are already positive about the place even before they get out of the car. The bonding of buyer to property has already begun. The challenging part is over because, with few exceptions, the inside of a house is usually a direct reflection of the outside. We just need to open the front door and let the property sell itself.

The Propitious Path to Your Door

Buyers can also begin to fall in love with a particular property as they walk up the front path. Some houses have such charm that it oozes out the front door and spills into the yard. I mention this again because, as buyers discover after previewing many houses, the front yard usually mirrors the way the home has been maintained on the inside.

Some owners have a knack for staging a property for sale — and this is a good thing. However, cosmetic touches like fresh paint and new wallpaper can mask serious structural flaws such as water stains or settling cracks (which you may not discover until the next good rain). But most sellers, who have done outstanding landscaping on the front yard, have probably maintained the house beautifully on the inside as well.

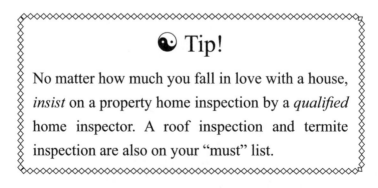

☯ Tip!

No matter how much you fall in love with a house, *insist* on a property home inspection by a *qualified* home inspector. A roof inspection and termite inspection are also on your "must" list.

A beautiful front yard attracts benevolent chi and buyers. Well-maintained, colorful plants, shrubs, flowers, and a manicured lawn go a long way toward bringing a smile to a buyer's face as well as raise the chi significantly.

- ☯ A meandering front pathway to the mouth of chi is a definite feng shui plus — this allows the chi to slow down so that buyers can savor the approach to the porch and front door.

- ☯ A pathway that is wider at the street and that tapers gently to the porch gets extra feng shui points. This wider-at-the-front design helps "gather in" the chi and funnels it to the front door.

- ☯ An expansive, broad front porch, preferably sheltered by a roof or arbor which allows the chi (and your guests) to relax and anticipate the interior.

- ☯ Steps leading up to the porch elevate the chi and set the property off from being on street level. The broader the steps the better. This allows benevolent energy to move slowly and easily up to the mouth of chi.

Straight walkways give a more formal and rigid feeling to a yard. The energy from the street wants to move quickly in a straight path creating a sha arrow toward the mouth of chi. Lush bedding plants loaded with blossoms that spill over the straight edges will help correct straight sha chi paths.

A meandering path is an excellent feng shui treatment for walkways.
Photos: Anne Czajka

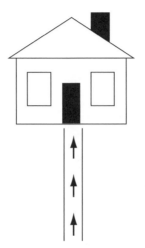

Straight and narrow pathways are sha arrows aiming at the front door.

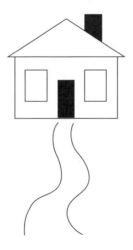

Curved pathways are energetically welcoming. Walkways that are wider at the street help gather in the chi.

The porch is a transition area from the front yard to the home's interior, and as such is an important place for the buyer to relax and enjoy the setting while the agent removes the key from the lock box, or waits for the seller to open the front door. It is here that buyers continue to form impressions of the property, and smart sellers will spend a lot of time and energy on the porch as a staging area for the rest of the house.

A rusty screen door, hanging cobwebs, old newspapers tossed in the corner of a porch in desperate need of sweeping, a tarnished and wobbly door knob, dirty door mat, dusty porch light hanging askew, paint peeling on the front door — are all strong indications that the interior of the house needs lots of cleaning and probably structural work as well.

The alternative image includes a freshly painted front door, shiny brass door knob, immaculate door mat, sparkling porch light, fresh color bowls of blooming flowers on either side of the door, and perhaps a fountain to massage the senses while you wait for your agent to open the door. You get the picture. In either case, the stage has been set and you have formed your first impressions.

The River of No Financial Return

If you are looking for a fixer-upper and the front yard and porch are a sorry sight, you have probably come to the right place. Hoping to reduce the price because of all the work that is needed is a thrifty thought, but there is a point at which your returns will diminish significantly.

If the house is just rundown, yet has great feng shui in other ways, proceed with common sense and extreme caution. Do not let yourself be talked into a "bargain" that will be a never-ending sinkhole for your cash. You are the one who will do all the work, not your agent or well-meaning brother-in-law who thinks it is a steal. If the property is rundown and has poor feng shui, it is no bargain, so get back in the car.

Your Front Door —
the Wondrous *Mouth of Chi*

Remember that feng shui is all about energy, so pay special attention to the energetic implications of the front door, also referred to earlier as the "mouth of chi." For feng shui reasons it is very important that you first enter any house you are considering for purchase through the main door so you can experience the movement of chi the way energy and blessings will come to you from the street. Be sure your real estate agent knows this. Even if it is more convenient to come through a side door where the lock box is placed, ask the agent to come around and open the mouth of chi for you.

The front door is where all good energy, fortunate blessings, and abundance of every delightful kind enter your home. Even though some houses have more than one entrance, consider the mouth of chi to be the door the architect designed to be the main door.

If you want to check that the main door faces one of your Positive Personal Directions (and I highly recommend that you do), this is the time to do it. See the Special Supplement toward the end of this book.

It is not great feng shui for *the driveway of your neighbor* directly across the street to be pointing at your front door. The continual backing up of their cars in line with your mouth of chi is not energetically advisable. A further consideration is the constant opening and closing of their garage is like a gaping mouth that you have to look into from your front porch; this is not the most auspicious or pleasing view, to say the least.

Can You See Me Now?

Beware of properties where the *front door and porch are not visible from the street.* Sometimes the mouth of chi is on the side of the house; this is not the greatest feng shui design because the beneficial chi has to turn a corner to find you. In cases like this hopefully the entrance is visible, with either a "welcome" plaque mounted on the closest front wall or some other equally clear indicator showing guests, the firemen, and good chi how to find you.

Sometimes the front door, even when facing the street, is hidden behind walls, porticos, or design features at the front of the house that totally block the door from view. In the case of living at a T or a Y-junction, you know that "hiding" the main door may be the only way to deal with unwanted sha energy. However, this is not the best scenario, because the good chi is blocked as well.

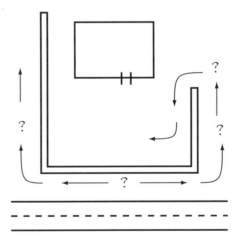

*Walls or hedges completely blocking the mouth of chi
make it difficult for abundance and blessings to find you.*

It is important in cases such as these that the house numbers are large and prominently displayed, and even lit up at night. Homes with a hidden front porch and main door need to have great feng shui in many other areas to overcome this major energetic challenge.

That Lucky Ole' Sun

The aspect of sunlight throughout a house is often one of the last things a buyer will consider. However, I encourage you to think about how the sun passes over the house you are considering purchasing. Buyers will have their own individual preferences (remember the yin/yang comfort zone example from Chapter 3). Some clients prefer a darker, more subdued house. However, I have found over my many years of showing property, that a majority of buyers prefer a sunny home with plenty of natural light.

Skylights are a wonderful solutions for dark spaces. Rooms that are typically in need of skylights are interior bathrooms, laundry rooms, large walk-in closets, and hallways. Building codes require bedrooms to have windows and most other rooms will have ample exterior light. It is not only expensive to put skylights or "solar tubes" in an already existing dwelling, but it may also compromise the structural integrity of a roof. Skylights can also be prone to leaks if not properly installed or caulked. Walking on a roof to install a skylight is not good for shingles or tiles.

Despite all these challenges, skylights and the beauty they bring to the interior of a dwelling are worth the risks and added cost! They add significant value to the house, and will repay you handsomely when you sell.

Not only are dark rooms more expensive to live in because of the rising costs of electricity, but dark spaces are also depressing to the spirit. To lift your chi, stay in the light and enjoy! The sun's pathway over a home is important to the comfort of the inhabitants. We are no longer cave dwellers; we emerged from that dark, uncomfortable existence long ago. Why go back? As we progress through the various rooms in the house on our "feng shui tour," keep that lucky ole' sun in mind.

The Entry Way — Keep the Chi Moving

When buyers are first ushered into a home with great feng shui in the front yard and porch, it can be a magical moment. The open and uncrowded entry way where the chi is lifted and feels light, should continue to carry out the good feelings experienced at the front door. Some pointers that will reinforce good feng shui principles at the entry are:

- ☯ Stairs should not greet you as you open the front door.

- ☯ A bathroom, the kitchen, (and definitely the refrigerator) should not be visible from the front door.

- ☯ A dark, narrow entry way tends to stifle chi.

- ☯ Well-lit, open entry spaces are best (mirrors and skylights work wonders).

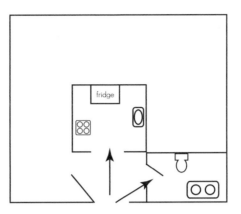

The refrigerator and the toilet should not be visible from the entry.

What if there is no entry and the floor plan deposits guests right into the living room, dining area, kitchen, or family area? As far as feng shui is concerned, there are no terribly adverse consequences — you just are where you are!

From a gracious living standpoint, a foyer or entry adds a dimension of heightened ambience. Your guests have a place to decompress and adjust to the chi of the home before heading off into the living room, family room, or wherever you intend to visit together.

When there is an entry or foyer, look to the bagua layout and determine into which Life Aspiration you are entering. According to Black Sect feng shui, if the main entry door (as you look at the house) is:

- ☯ *centered* across the front of the home, your entry will be in the *Career* Aspiration.

- ☯ on the *left*, you enter into *Wisdom and Knowledge*;

- ☯ on the *right*, the entry is in the *Helpful People* area.

Look at the bagua positioned over a floor plan and imagine that the nine (eight plus the central tai chi) Life Aspirations are circles of energy that will fill the space. An example of this method is shown below. Use whichever technique works best for you; they accomplish the same results allowing you to easily see where the Life Aspirations fit into any structure.

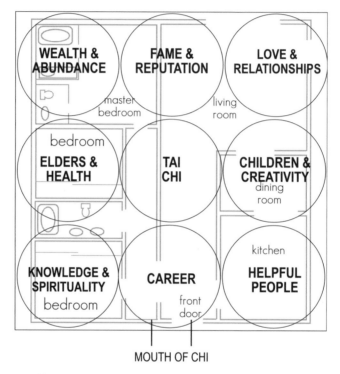

Placement of bagua over floor plan using circles to indicate Life Aspirations.

Note in the example above that the front left bedroom is in front of the home mid-line. You will come across homes with this and other challenges as you do your previewing. A good use for this bedroom would be an active (yang) office where clients visit. Using it as a bedroom (yin) sleeping area would place the occupant close to the stressful chi from the street traffic.

Living, Family, and Great Rooms

From the entry way, the floor plan usually leads into the living room. These days we have the "great room" concept where the formal living room has been waived in favor of a more informal living-family room combination. Great rooms often will have a fireplace and provide a more relaxed atmosphere for guests.

Floor plans having a formal living room are fine too. Older or more traditionally designed homes will usually have a separate, formal living room. This interior space gives a somewhat more refined feel and is often devoted to less familiar guests. (I always think of the Avon lady visiting my mother.)

Both living rooms and great rooms are considered yang functioning spaces because both family activities and entertaining guests take place here. Good chi circulation is especially important here due to the many functions that the great room, living room, and family room serve. For good chi flow these spaces should:

- be in *front of the mid-line* of the home
- have as much natural light as possible
- have easy access to the kitchen
- have a good view to the outside
- provide enough space for family as well as quiet activities.

Although family rooms probably started with the more informal living style on the West Coast, they have definitely been growing in popularity in the East. They have evolved from not only being the escape from the formal living room, but also the transition from the living room to the great room. Here is where everyone can plop down to watch television, read in a quiet corner, play a board game, or snooze on the sofa.

Family rooms are usually adjacent to the kitchen, and will frequently contain a dining area. For families with children, this is the place where toys can be left out or stored easily in baskets; magazines, books, and favorite reading materials are within easy access. If asked to enter the family room, guests understand that this more informal space will be relaxed in nature.

The Feng Shui Dining Room

Along with the kitchen, the dining room is possibly one of the happiest rooms in the house. It is one of the home's yang areas and lots of activities go on here. If you are the entertaining type, this room will be of particular importance.

Many floor plans have the kitchen sharing space with a dining area. Often, houses do not have a formal dining room, and many buyers don't require one. This is a personal consideration. It is nice to have a designated eating space for the family and guests separated a bit from the kitchen, so that pans left in the sink are not visible during dinner.

For good feng shui the dining room should be:

- ☯ positioned in *front of the mid-line* of the house
- ☯ large enough to accommodate your table and at least four chairs.
- ☯ spacious enough for the chi to easily circulate around the table and for guests to sit comfortably and get up without backing a chair into a wall
- ☯ easily accessible to the kitchen

☯ sunny and filled with light during the day

☯ designed with a window for a pleasant view

☯ able to have the table placed in such a way so that chi from opposite doors does not "cut" across the table.

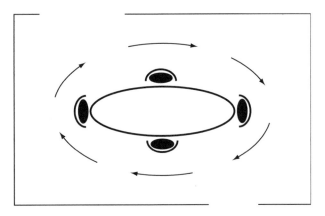

Chi needs to circulate easily around the dining table.

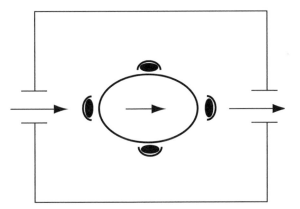

Be careful not to place your dining table in the line of two opposing doors allowing sha chi to cut across the table.

The Kitchen: the Most Significant Yang Room

From a feng shui perspective, the kitchen is also a yang functioning room and, next to the yin master bedroom, it is the most important energetic room consideration in the house. The kitchen, traditionally the center of "home and hearth," should be positioned in front of the home's mid-line.

It is especially advantageous if the kitchen:

- ☯ is not seen from the front door or entry way

- ☯ does not share a wall with a bathroom

- ☯ allows the cook to face the door while cooking and preparing food

- ☯ has plenty of natural light

- ☯ does not have a bathroom located on the floor directly above, especially over the stove.

Master Bedroom: the Most Important Yin Space

Considered the most important feng shui space in the home, the master bedroom is where the owners of the dwelling spend one-third of their lives. It is a very yin room and is best positioned behind the mid-line of the home and in the far right or southwest corner (Love and Romance Aspiration). The master bedroom provides the Three Rs of feng shui — Rest, Romance, and Relaxation — here the body is refreshed, the spirit renewed, and the senses re-awakened to begin each new day.

In many modern homes the master bedroom often has an adjacent master bath designed *without* a separating door between the rooms; the chi from the two spaces frequently flow together having no real boundaries. To say nothing of compromising privacy, from a feng shui standpoint, it is far better to have the sleeping space physically separated from the bathroom (where the chi is dramatically drained away) by a door, or at the very least, a curtain that defines the spaces. Be sure that the view from the master bed does not look directly into the bathroom.

Try to find a floor plan with a master bedroom that:

- ☯ is separated by a door from the master bath

- ☯ is well behind the house mid-line

- ☯ is preferably at the very rear of the home

- ☯ is ideally located in the southwest or far right corner of the floor plan

- ☯ that does not have a bathroom (and especially a toilet) behind the wall where the master bed will be located

- ☯ allows for bed placement without the bed facing the door

- ☯ does not have doors on either side facing into the bed

- ☯ does not have a bathroom overhead on the second story

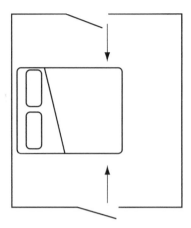

Bed with doors opening on both sides is energetically disturbing.
Chi cuts right across the bed.

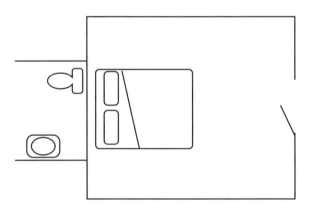

Bed sharing the same wall with a toilet — chi draining
much too close to sleeping occupants.

An additional reminder to avoid in the master bedroom is the "coffin position" for the bed mentioned in Chapter 4. Be sure that your bed is not placed so that the feet are pointing directly out the door. Give special thought to the energy you feel in the master bedroom. Spend at least a few minutes alone there so that you can get in touch with how the space will nurture you.

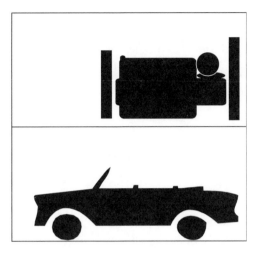

Having a garage under a bedroom subjects the sleeper to excess amounts of sha chi from movement of cars, noxious odors, etc.

Tell Me Your True Feelings, Darlin'

Remember that intuition is on your side. With practice, intuition will guide you to what is best for you in any situation or environment. House hunting is no exception, and wife and husband or partners must be extremely open and clear with each other about their feelings, especially in this most important master bedroom.

The woman may have a strong positive sensation in the bedroom where her partner may have an opposite reaction. Both these feelings will probably not go away but only grow stronger as time passes. I would recommend against buying a house where one partner feels any questionable energetic reaction or serious negativity. If you begin to pick up on any negative energy, try to find the source: a neighboring window that diminishes your privacy, a sloping ceiling or heavy overhead beams. (These will be covered in detail in Chapter 10.)

Many negative influences can be easily changed into positive ones with paint, window coverings or other decorative treatment. However some cannot, and will be with the house until you move. Taking the time to assess your feelings throughout the house and especially in the master bedroom now, will be time well spent.

Bathrooms - Where It All Goes Down the Drain

We need 'em, we love 'em, and yet bathrooms have special feng shui negative considerations because this is where waste and water drains away from the house in significant amounts. Since water represents abundance, benevolent blessings, and riches of all kinds, we have a feng shui two-edged sword when it comes to bathrooms.

In days of old, out-houses were the perfect feng shui answer. Not only were they outside, but they did not have flowing water. However, I would be the last to suggest giving up my delightful bathroom in trade for an outhouse! A bathroom located in the center of the home is a serious feng shui no-no, and I strongly discourage purchasing a house with such a floor plan since the tai chi energy of the home and family is continually flushed away.

Also, avoid a bathroom located in the southeast or far left corner of the floor plan. This is the Wealth Aspiration of the bagua, and it is unwise to tempt fate when it comes to money leaving the household. Keep the good chi in, especially in the area related to good fortune and family finances.

In a two-story house, it is not great feng shui to have a bathroom positioned over the entry, master bedroom, or kitchen for reasons you are already aware of — the excessive, negative draining chi will come down over your head in these important areas. Bathrooms are not a good idea overhead in any area, but some rooms are more significant than others.

Make sure that a bathroom:

- is not in the center of the house
- does not share a wall with the toilet behind the master bed
- is not in the southeast (Wealth) or far left corner of the house
- is not in the southwest (Love & Romance) or far right corner of the floor plan.
- does not share a wall with the kitchen
- is not visible from the front door or entry
- has plenty of ventilation from a fan or a skylight (if it does not have a window)

The Laundry Room — Oh Darn, More Drains

Certainly one of the less significant rooms in the house, and often saved for a corner in the garage, the laundry area has feng shui considerations — water and good chi drain from the house here also. Although not as serious as bathrooms draining chi away, laundry areas need special consideration too. For convenience sake, many buyers like to have a laundry room inside the house. These days, besides having a washer and dryer, there is often a laundry tub in this space — another drain!

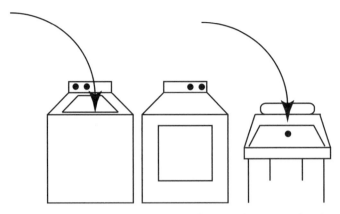

More drains in the laundry room... down and out goes the chi.

In a perfect feng shui world, the laundry room would not be in the center of the house (you already know why) or in the Wealth Aspiration (Southeast corner). Other than those areas, you can feel pretty secure as you suds your duds.

The Garage — Where All the Stuff Is Out of Sight, Out of Mind

When teaching feng shui, I laughingly refer to the garage as the "storage unit" because in the countless properties I have shown over the years that is what the garage has become. When we have filled every cupboard and closet, stuffed the attic and the basement, the garage is our next depository for all the stuff we collect.

Hopefully, you will use the opportunity of moving to reduce and recycle all the things you have carted around from place to place. This is your big chance! Don't bring your old clutter to your new home because clutter is stuck chi that energetically weighs you down.

In homes of the past, the garage, if there was one, was detached from the house — but not today. Garages (often for three or four cars) are not only attached to the main house, they often physically support a family room or a master bedroom on the floor above.

From an energetic standpoint of chi, garages are a major source of noxious energy from vehicles moving in and out at various times throughout the day and night. If the house is a single level, the only question is which room (or rooms) is directly adjacent to the garage, since that area will receive the energetic buffeting from automotive chi. From what we have already discussed, you know that having a garage adjacent to a master bedroom is not good feng shui.

Walls Have Little Bearing with Chi

Below are included some typical floor plans with the bagua superimposed. As you study each one, remember that the bagua is an energy template and like water, will fit the shape of whatever space it is given.

Walls have little bearing where feng shui is concerned — the chi of a particular Life Aspiration will energetically move through physical barriers and occupy a given area no matter how many walls are in the way. Walls will guide the chi, but not block it. Where Life Aspirations meet, the energy of each blends together like chalk colors that can be smudged into a gently blended transition.

Each Life Aspiration makes up one-ninth (including the central tai chi) of the home's energy and space. Remember the lo-shu magic square from Chapter 2? With practice you will soon easily begin to place the bagua in each prospective house. Like learning a new language, it is fun to realize, "This is my Relationships Aspiration and over there is my Helpful People Aspiration."

Consider What Is Missing

Hopefully, in the large picture, your potential lot shape is a regular square or rectangle. Boot, cleaver, and triangular lot shapes all have symbolic energetic challenges of "missing areas" and should be avoided. On a smaller scale, if a floor plan is irregular (not a square or a rectangle) it is likely to have a missing area or a "projection."

On this smaller scale, missing areas are serious energetic bagua "holes" where a Life Aspiration (or part of one) is not present in the floor plan. Energetically, this situation needs to be remedied, usually with a simple procedure of "completing" where the exterior walls would have come together to make a finished corner. To complete, place a grounding element such as a light post, boulder, tree, bench, birdbath, or gazing ball on a pedestal, or any solid design element of your choice. A light (such as a pole porch light) or other symbol of illumination (such as a tiki torch) placed at the spot where the walls would have intersected, are excellent solutions.

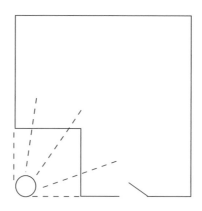

The point of a floor plan needing energetic completion on the exterior can be illuminated by a light fixture or grounded by a gazing ball, substantial plant, bench, etc.

If the missing area is allowed to remain incomplete, the feng shui consequences result in beneficial chi not being able to fill that space, resulting in lost energy to that kua. Missing areas in the Wealth, Relationships, and Career Life Aspirations can have detrimental consequences, and feng shui students will want to remedy these conditions.

Having a *projection,* on the other hand, allows additional chi to circulate and bring extra abundance of energy to that area. Missing areas and projections are determined by whether they measure less than 50 percent of the wall in question.

Two examples:

1. *A wall measures 30 feet in length. The missing corner is 10 feet long (50% would be 15 feet). Because the corner is less than 1/2 the length of the primary wall it is considered "missing." The corner needs to be "completed" on the exterior where the two walls would have met.*

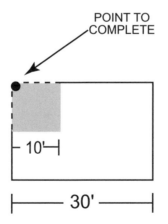

Missing area is shaded in gray. This needs to be energetically "completed" outside the house where walls would have met.

2. *A wall measures 25 feet in length. The corner of that wall projects out 9 feet. Because the length is less than 1/2 of the primary wall it is considered to be a "projection." (50% of 25 feet = 12.5 feet) This 9-foot corner projection allows a greater amount of chi to circulate in that area — great!*

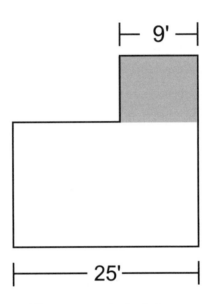

The projection is shaded gray.
Projections in a floor plan allow more circulation of beneficial chi.

When the shape of the floor plan is regular, as in a square or rectangle, the bagua can easily fit over the shape without creating missing corners. The more irregular the shape of the floor plan, the more missing areas and projections show up.

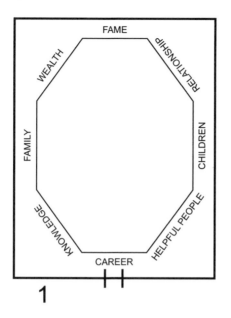

The bagua fits completely over a rectangle or square floor plan.

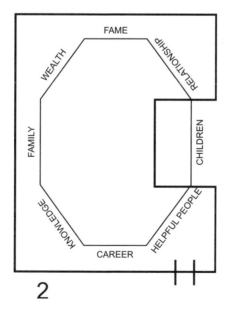

When a section of the floor plan is missing, the bagua energy in that Life Aspiration is depleted.

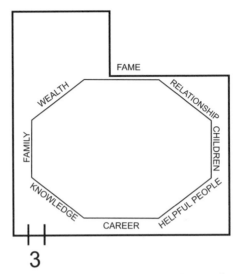

3

When there is a projection beyond the regular bagua shape, the chi has more room to circulate.

In a perfect world of feng shui, all floor plans would be square or rectangular. Figure 1 shows how the entire bagua easily fits over the regular shape — the feng shui ideal. Figure 2 illustrates the missing area in the Children and Creativity Life Aspiration. This is a very common feng shui challenge, and often there are several missing areas in a floor plan. Figure 3 shows a projection above and beyond the bagua energy template over the floor plan — room for more chi to enter this area.

From early Chinese feng shui practice until today, a regular-shaped parcel has been preferred because the energetic template of the bagua can be applied easily without having to deal with missing Life Aspirations. All the areas of the bagua are equally important, but no one wants to have a missing Wealth or Romance area!

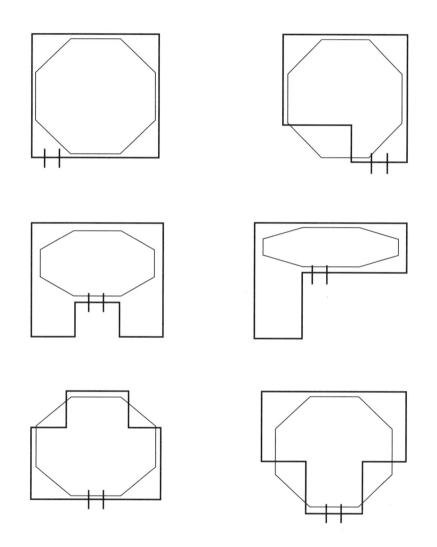

Typical floor plans showing how superimposed bagua stretches and shrinks to fit individual designs and spaces.

Practice Floor Plans

At the end of this section there are sample floor plans where you can pencil in the bagua and Life Areas you have learned. Take time to practice with these before you go out looking at houses. I especially want you to be able to locate the Wealth, Relationships, and Career Life Sectors. The rest of the bagua will be easy to learn once you have these three areas memorized.

- ☯ If you walk through the front door located in the *center front* of the house, you are in Career.

- ☯ The Wealth area is located at the *far rear left*,

- ☯ and the Relationships sector is in the *back far right*.

These are important to be able to recognize because ideally you do not want a bathroom located in either Wealth, Relationships, or Career. Likewise, there should not be a missing area in any of these three.

A few more tips as you do this exercise:

- ☯ Whatever areas are under the roofline should be included in the bagua.

- ☯ Porches would not be considered as part of the bagua unless they are enclosed, have substantial walls, and are under the main roof.

- ☯ Breezeways or un-enclosed passageways between the house and garage are not included.

- ☯ *For our purposes at this point, do not worry about the Five Elements or colors associated with the bagua and Life Aspirations.* Focus on where the main door is located and apply the bagua accordingly.

Most of these floor plans are not regular in shape. They will have "missing areas" or "projections" which were discussed in Chapter 8. That is the point of this practice — to help you become familiar with laying the bagua over all types of floor plans. Notice especially how the missing areas will affect the Life Aspirations. Label the Life Aspirations in pencil so that you can more easily identify which ones are affected by being "missing."

The following floor plan shapes are intended as additional practice for you. Follow these steps:

- ☯ Lay the bagua over each floor plan.

- ☯ Next, draw and label each Life Aspiration

- ☯ Be sure you place the tai chi as an equal area in the center. This will give you nine equal circles or ovals of the house's energy pattern.

- ☯ Using the main door as your guide (if it is centrally located), that area is Career. To the left of the main door is Knowledge and to the right is Helpful People.

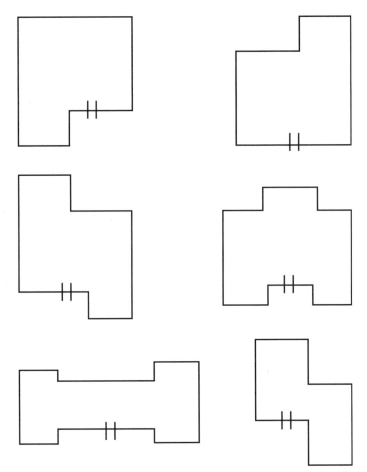

Draw the octagonal bagua shape over these irregular floor plans; then sketch in the eight Life Aspirations and central tai chi.

You will soon get the hang of it and find yourself feeling where the different Life Aspirations are in any floor plan. As you are looking at many houses in one day, it is hard to remember the placement of all those rooms when you get home. Get into the habit of sketching the floor plan for any property you really like while you are there at the house.

Chapter 9 — Check Your *Chi* List

Front yard, walkway, and porch:

___ Are the porch and front door visible from the street? (+)

___ Does the front path to the main door curve gently? (+)
or is it straight and rigid? (-)

___ Is the porch slightly elevated? (+)

___ Is the porch large with room for a fountain? (+)

___ Is the porch sheltered by a roof or arbor? (+)

___ Does your front door look directly across to the neighbor's
driveway and garage? (-)

Front door (mouth of chi):

___ Is the front door strong, solid, and in good condition? (+)

___ Is the threshold solid? (+)

___ Is the doorknob firm to the grip? (+)

___ Does the key work without difficulty? (+)

Entry/Foyer:

___ Is the entry open and light (+) or small and dark? (-)

___ Can you add a skylight if necessary? (+)

___ Can you see the kitchen or a bathroom from the entry? (-)

___ Is the size of the entry adequate for chi to circulate easily before
entering the rest of the house? (+)

Living Room / Great Room

___ Is the living room naturally light and spacious? (+)

___ Is there a window with a view? (+)

___ Is there room for chi to circulate for various activities? (+)

Dining Room:

___ Is the dining room adjacent to the kitchen? (+)

___ Is it naturally lit with a window and a view? (+)

___ Is there adequate room for chi to move around the table and chairs allowing plenty of room for guests to move easily? (+)

Family Room:

___ Is the family room adjacent to kitchen and eating area? (+)

___ Does it have adequate space for various activities? (+)

___ Does it have natural sunshine? (+)

Kitchen:

___ Can the cook see the kitchen door while preparing food (+) and cooking at the stove? (+)

___ Is there a bathroom adjacent to the kitchen? (-)

___ Is the kitchen in front of the home's mid-line? (+)

___ Is there a bathroom on the floor above the kitchen? (-)

___ Is there a toilet on the floor above the stove? (-)

Master Bedroom:

___ Is the master bedroom located at the far rear right (or southwest) corner of the house? (+)

___ Is the master bedroom placed behind the house's mid-line? (+)

___ Is the master bedroom bed on the same wall as an adjacent bathroom or a toilet? (-)

___ Is the master bath located inside the master bedroom? (-)

___ Is there a closeable door separating the bedroom from the bathroom? (+)

Bathrooms:

__ Is a bathroom in the center or tai chi area of the house? (- -)
This is a feng shui deal breaker. Keep looking!

__ Is a bathroom located in the Wealth Area (southeast) or Love and
Romance Area (southwest) of the home's bagua? (-)

__ Is a bathroom adjacent to the kitchen? (-)

Laundry Room:

__ Is the laundry room in the center or tai chi of the house? (-)

Garage:

__ Is the garage detached from the main house? (+)

__ If attached to the main house, is the entire house on one level? (+)

__ Is the garage adjacent to a yang function room? (+)

__ Is the garage adjacent to a yin function room such as the master
bedroom or a study? (-)

__ If a two level home, is the garage located under the master
bedroom? (-)

Doors, Windows, Stairs, Beams, the Works!

*Elizabeth and Russ have been looking at houses for three months; they had no idea searching for a new place would be such hard work. Their great agent, Willow, calls every time a new listing comes up that sounds good, but nothing they have seen so far is close to being **the** one.*

Elizabeth, an artist, has taken several feng shui classes and has read many books on the subject. Her husband Russ, an architect and also an artist, has not had feng shui training, but trusts Elizabeth's judgment when it comes to criteria for their next house. Russ is the cook in the family and his only request is a functional kitchen. They both know that harmony and balance within their living space is of the utmost importance and are willing to be patient until Willow comes up with just the right home.

Yesterday they saw four houses. The first one has several great features, but has a staircase directly in front of the main door. The second property also has many good points, but has massive dark beams throughout the house. The next place has a very good floor plan with the exception of a spiral staircase in the center of the house. The fourth property got close; that one had a bathroom in the far left, southeast corner that Elizabeth called the "Wealth" area. She knows that each of these problems is a specific and serious feng shui challenge.

Elizabeth is aware that some problems present a greater energetic burden to correct than others, yet so far the advantages do not outweigh the disadvantages. She tells Russ they are getting close, but the right place is still out there.

Willow is fascinated at how much she is learning about feng shui. She has heard a lot about applying it to real estate, but these are her first clients who are very knowledgeable. It all makes sense to her, and now saves her time because she knows what kind of houses not to show Elizabeth and Russ.

This morning there was a house on the broker tour in a great location that felt wonderful. It did not have any of the feng shui problems they had found in earlier properties, and Willow was excited when she called Russ and Elizabeth. They made an appointment for that afternoon.

Driving through the neighborhood, they noticed it was clean and pleasant with mature trees lining the streets. As they pulled up and got out of the car, Russ noticed how carefully the front yard had been maintained. The owner let them in and then went into the backyard. Willow guided them through the house and Elizabeth was pleased to see how clean and bright the home was.

The rooms were sparsely furnished so they were able to get a sense of how their own pieces of furniture would fit in each room. The master bedroom was in the southwest, far right corner of the floor plan, which pleased Elizabeth. "This is our feng shui Romance area," she said happily. "Great!"

Stairs to the second story were offset, away from the front door; no feng shui problem here. The kitchen layout allowed Russ to face the door when cooking — another plus. The upstairs bedrooms, each filled with natural light, would be ideal for their art workrooms.

Willow could sense things were going well for her clients in this house. The subtle, yet important feng shui criteria were all in place. The house felt wonderful to all of them. Russ and Elizabeth decided they wanted to make a full-price offer — they did not want to lose this one.

Doors — Portals of Power

As you already know, doors are considered entrances (and exits) for chi, especially the front door, or the mouth of chi.

☯ Tip!

All the doors of the house and especially the main entry should be in good condition without squeaky hinges. The primary door needs to have a solid threshold and a firm handle or knob that does not feel loose to the grip. Keys should work easily and glass inserts in doors should sparkle.

Problems with doors are certainly not deal breakers, and are all easily corrected and upgraded. If the front door frame is tweaked and out of plumb, that is significant — metaphorically if the mouth of chi is "out of whack" put this item on your list of "musts to fix." If the rest of the house is great do not forget about it after you have moved in!

In addition to exterior doors, interior doors are also significant, and may require simple energetic remedies. Check for the following:

Arguing doors are doors leading into different rooms that bang into each other when opened at the same time. When this happens the harmony of the space is disrupted. If one door needs to close first, the remaining door "loses" the argument. In the meantime, your family has to endure the continual battle. An easy fix is to make sure only one door opens at a time. Another would be to hang a faceted crystal from the ceiling between where the two doors usually collide.

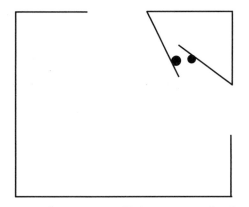

Arguing doors continually bang into each other.

Biting doors are slightly offset from each other down a hallway; they constitute a "bad (dental) bite" and appear poorly aligned. This creates an imbalance that the brain constantly tries to fix, but cannot. A simple solution for biting doors is to position mirrors next to each door to create the illusion that each doorway is aligned with the one on the opposite wall.

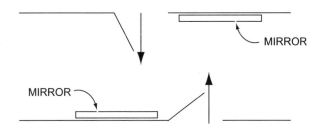

Biting doors are offset and energetically misaligned.

Another feng shui solution for these energetic clashes is to hang a faceted crystal to disperse negative chi and keep the chi moving past the disquieting area. Coming out of a room and seeing only a portion of a door across the hall can create a subtle sense of unevenness and the feeling that you need corrective lenses.

Contrary doors open directly into a wall or a very small portion of a room. As you open a contrary door you step into a section of an adjoining wall or in some way have to move around the door in order to get into the main part of the room. This situation makes you feel blocked and inhibited and is an example of poor room design.

A contrary door opens into a wall.

The best solution is to change the hinges to the opposite side of the door jam to reverse the door making it open into the most expansive part of the room. If, for some reason changing the hinges is not an option, place a mirror or picture of a lovely scene on the wall, so that when opening that door, people are not energetically cramped by a "brick wall" effect. This also encourages the chi to keep moving into the main part of the room.

Pierced heart doors are at least three doors in a row that open into rooms in a straight line. The energy moving through these aligned doors makes one feel targeted, especially if your bed or desk is directly in the "line of fire." A crystal hung within each room to slow the chi down would be your first feng shui line of defense. However, houses with this poor design probably have other worse feng shui challenges that would be an energetic turnoff.

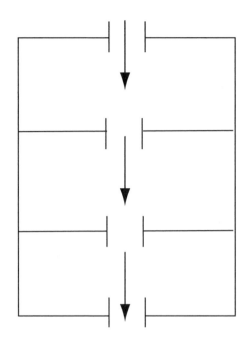

Pierced heart doors make positioning furniture an energetic challenge.

In general, try to avoid any awkward door placement such as a confined hallway with three or more doors. This tends to create energetic confusion, indecisiveness, and inhibits freely flowing chi. "Pocket" doors that slide into a wall space can be excellent structural remedies for a home with this type of situation. However, they are usually inserted when the wall is originally built, which requires a major remodel after the fact, probably not your first choice.

All doors should be able to open as widely as possible against the nearest wall in order to allow the greatest amount of chi to enter the room, representing fortunate blessings and opportunities coming into our lives. This good chi should not be obstructed by any built-in bookcase, furniture, or stored items (clutter) on the floor behind.

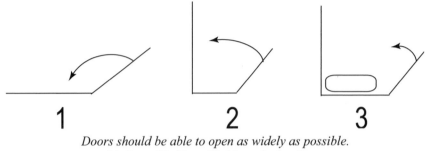

Doors should be able to open as widely as possible.
#1 Best, #2 Okay, #3 Move the bookcase.

A very common design challenge is the *front door / back door line of sight: a direct view from the front door out the rear.* Like a fast moving river of chi that rushes through and then is gone, the all-important chi energy wants to dart straight through, thus eliminating the possibility of energy circulating gently and completely throughout the house first. The remedy for such a floor plan is to hang a faceted crystal in front of the rear door, which will deflect the chi as well as slow it down. A table with a vase of flowers will accomplish the same thing.

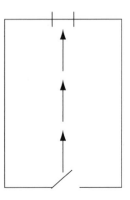

Direct Front Door / Back Door Line of Sight

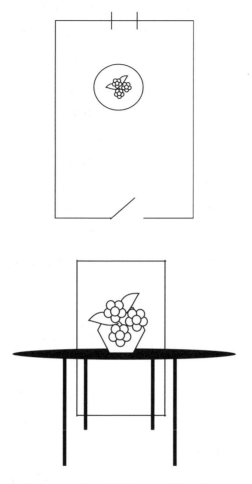

When front and back doors are aligned, place a table, plant, or crystal to block the chi from leaving through the back door.

A Room with a View — Priceless

A breathtaking view is priceless and raises the home's value enormously. City ordinances are passed to prevent views from being blocked, and buyers will pay more for a home with an amazing view, especially of water (beauty and abundance). When a home is lucky enough to have a fabulous view, the windows, obviously, are what show it off. Windows are the picture frames through which we gaze on the beauty of nature, thus their placement becomes especially significant. Not putting a window where there is a stunning view misses the whole feng shui point.

Years ago I previewed a home located on a prominent hillside overlooking the ocean. For some unknown reason the builder had not put windows on the ocean side, and the house was just like any other house back in the hills. Oddly, the sellers did not seem to understand how important an ocean view was to support the price they were asking. The house remained unsold for several years, just waiting for a buyer who planned to put in windows facing the sea.

Windows, especially large ones, are also places where chi can leave the dwelling. It can be a feng shui challenge to have a large window directly opposite the mouth of chi because the energy moves directly out without first circulating throughout the house.

Windows should:

- ☯ open easily (repair those that are painted shut)
- ☯ have locking mechanisms that work effortlessly
- ☯ not have cracks or BB shot holes.

These items have health, safety, and feng shui implications. If any of these conditions exist in your prospective house, ask the seller to correct them as a condition of sale prior to close of escrow.

☯ Tip!

In feng shui, glass represents the Water Element, and contributes to the Elemental balance within a room. A living room, for example, with many large windows may be over-weighted towards Water. Chapter 5 discussed how the different Cycles of Elements nourish, control, or reduce each other.

The Nourishing Cycle shows how the Metal Element "holds" and thus supports Water. To elementally balance this, lighten up on the Metal Element and "dam" some of the abundant Water with a bit of the Earth Element.

This is easily accomplished with tile flooring, yellow or brown earth colors in throw pillows or in paintings. Planters (that contain soil), and any artwork representing mountains, deserts, or fields will bring Earth to the space.

Wood reduces Water, so adding plants and wood furniture would also help. The creative possibilities are endless.

Houses that have no back door or rooms without windows should be avoided. Fire and safety codes in most areas do not allow windowless rooms or houses without a secondary fire exit, but sometimes a few turn up, usually a result of owner-installed additions done without permits. As well as being a safety hazard, windowless rooms are cave-like and as such will harbor stagnant energy,.

In traditional feng shui, the windows of a house are considered to be the "voices" of the children and so are to be kept in lesser proportion to the exterior doors, considered to be the "voices" of the adults. Doors should always "carry more authority" and be larger than the windows. Otherwise it is believed that unruly children will rule the roost!

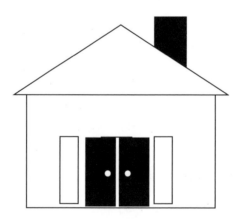

Windows (voices of the children) need to be in proportion to larger doors (voices of the adults). In this example the doors are bigger than the windows.

Stairs — Chi Flows down the Steps and out the Door

Although staircases are an inevitable condition of today's multistory house designs, there are important feng shui consequences of stairways. *Stairs are considered waterfalls of chi,* and it is vital that the chi of abundance and blessings that should circulate within the home does not flow straight out the door.

Sometimes a floor plan will have a stairway immediately in front of the main door, so that as you open the door the chi rushes out right past you.

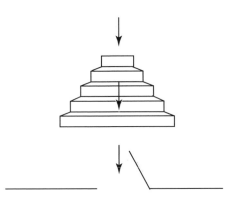

One of feng shui's biggest challenges:
the stairway facing the mouth of chi.

Another feng shui difficulty with an entry door that faces a stairway, is that your own inner chi can be confused, especially if you are new to the house. Do I go right, left, or up the stairs? Without knowing the floor plan of a house you are viewing, this design puts visitors into an energetic quandary.

Offset stairs (over to one side or the other from the main door) are fine — the chi will circulate first before finding the front door. The best advice is still to avoid purchasing a home with a floor plan having a front door directly facing a staircase.

If you have already fallen madly in love with a house that has an interior stairway facing the mouth of chi, the feng shui remedies would be to hang a faceted crystal sphere (or a crystal chandelier) directly in front of the staircase, and/or to place a circular rug in front of the stairs. This encourages the chi to circulate and slow down, somewhat mitigating the rush of energy out the door.

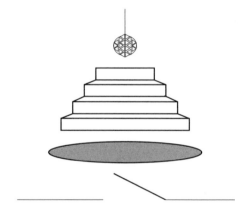

Circular area rug and / or a faceted crystal sphere will slow the chi.

Note: Faceted crystal spheres of various sizes are often used in solving feng shui challenges. Usually the rule is: "the bigger the problem, the bigger the crystal." Crystals are especially helpful in dispersing cutting or fast moving sha chi.

The sphere is more successful at this than other shapes of faceted crystals, and quartz crystals are a better choice than the lead variety. Quartz crystals can be harder to find as well as more expensive than lead ones; and if the quartz type aren't suited to your pocketbook, the lead ones will do.

Faceted crystal prisms are also useful in attracting beneficial chi and can act to "power up" or strengthen a Life Aspiration. They are also effective in "lifting" weighty or oppressive chi in cases such as sloping ceilings discussed later in this chapter.

Crystals represent the Metal Element and can help in balancing the Five Elements within a room (refer to Chapter 5). Crystals are not the solution for every problem, however, and it is always best to consult with an experienced feng shui practitioner if you have any doubts.

Stairs in other areas of the home are not so chi problematic; a landing midway up a flight of stairs is a positive feature. Any time there is a straight pathway, be it a driveway, walkway, hall, or staircase, the chi moves much too quickly. A physical feature such as a stair landing forces the energy to slow down.

Curved stairs combine yin and yang elements.

Curved stairways are visually appealing, graceful, and elegant, reminding us of Tara, the stately plantation home in the movie *Gone with the Wind.* On an energetic level, we find curved staircases beautiful because the yin curve balances the yang uprights and brings a refreshing change and a sense of balance from the 90 degree angles of most rooms. Feng shui is at work here. Curved staircases lend a sense of drama and romance to a room, especially a foyer or entry. Scarlet O'Hara would never have made a grand entrance down an ordinary straight staircase!

An easy way to energetically soften otherwise rigid lines of a straight staircase is to place lush plants next to the rising stairs – shorter ones in front and taller at back, having some of the leaves drape over the handrail or peek through the uprights. Another feng shui solution is to wind an ivy or pine bower (silk or artificial are fine) around the banister which will energetically soften the rigid chi of the straight stairs.

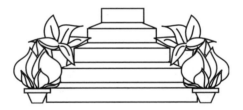

A simple treatment for a straight staircase giving a softened look.

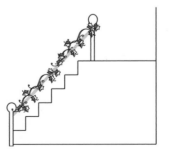

Ivy garland will soften rigid stairs and handrails.

Spiral staircases are quite another matter. They are considered "corkscrews of chi" that pull energy from above, down and away. The energetic solution for a spiral staircase is to put a substantial potted plant (a great looking silk plant will do) under the spiral to block the chi from funneling downward. *A spiral staircase located in the energetic center, or tai chi area of a house, is definitely not good feng shui and should be avoided.*

A spiral staircase can act like a corkscrew of chi.

Any stairs with open risers have the tendency to let the chi fall through the open spaces giving the feeling of floating instead of stepping on a confident path. The first solution would be to add the missing risers if possible; if risers are not an option, the alternative solution would be to place one or more large plants beneath the stairs to keep the chi from being lost through the openings.

Stairs with open risers allow chi to fall through.

A **Mandarin duck stairway** is one that goes both up and down from the main floor. The challenge with this design is that it confuses both people and good chi. Energetic indecision and bewilderment can take over and feng shui corrective measures are in order.

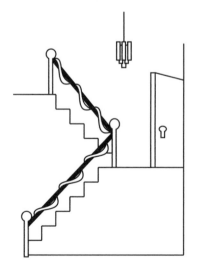

Mandarin Duck Stairway

Bringing the landing into prime focus with a prominent area rug, (preferably round or oval) allows the chi to relax and stay awhile. A sizeable faceted crystal prism or light fixture centered over the landing would be appropriate to further encourage the energy to linger.

Beams Will Weigh You Down

Overhead beams often need feng shui treatment, especially those painted a dark color. Be especially cautious of beams over a master bed (or anyone else's bed) as they are considered a potential cause for back problems or other physical ailments over time.

This condition is due to beams energetically "bearing down" on those below, being a source of energetic stress. Any stress, over time, will have effects on the body, much like a sharp sha corner that sends negative energy toward whatever is in its path. This physical effect takes place on an inner, subtle anatomy level; which, like water dripping over time, can wear down a stone.

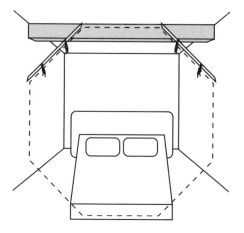

Overhead beams are energetic weights bearing down on those below.
Traditional remedy is bamboo flutes placed on bagua slant.

The traditional solution for massive overhead beams is to position two flutes, with the mouthpiece toward the bottom, on a forty-five degree angle (imitating the bagua shape), facing each other on the beam. This energetically lifts the chi and prevents its downward weighty effects. If this solution does not work with your decor, another easy fix to visually "lift" the beams is to paint them the same color as the ceiling and watch them fade away. Depending on size and height, faux finishes in a light color that match the ceiling are especially effective.

Pillars and Posts: Do Not Let Them Block Chi

Sometimes pillars or posts are structurally needed within a space. They are square or round depending on the interior design of the architect. Round pillars are a yin feature. They hold up the structure without emanating sha chi.

If the pillars are painted a color to match the walls of the room, they will tend to blend in and be much less obtrusive; faux finishes are especially effective. Another method is to simply place an attractive plant, with gently-shaped (not excessively pointed) leaves in front of the pillar which will visually remove the harsh corners.

> ## ☯ Tip!
>
> General rule: a round pillar is better than a square post because the four yang corners on the square posts will send sha chi into the room. If you multiply this cutting energy by the number of posts, you have a big dose of negative chi.

The best way to energetically erase a square post is to mirror all four sides, especially in a commercial setting. This is a bit more expensive, but the effect is amazing. More and more restaurants, department stores, and modern convention centers employ this technique, resulting in posts that energetically disappear as if by magic.

Ceilings — Energy from on High

Yes, ceilings too have energetic implications and although this is usually a minor feng shui adjustment, some ceilings can be a challenge. Most houses will have normal eight-foot ceilings (though older homes often have higher ones); second story bedrooms often have sloping ceilings from dormers or slanted rooflines.

Many newer condominiums and townhouses have sloping upstairs ceilings, usually in the bedrooms, thus caution is necessary for sleepers below. Energetically speaking, downward sloping ceilings are similar to massive beams that weigh you down with heavy energy. Consistently sleeping or working under a severely sloping ceiling can energetically contribute to headaches, back problems, malaise, digestive ailments, and various aches and pains.

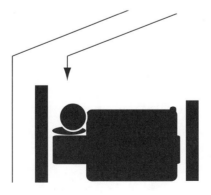

Bed under slanted ceiling brings weighty chi down on the sleeper.

Visually "erase" a sloping ceiling by painting it the same (preferably very light) color as the rest of the ceiling, instead of emphasizing it as a design element with a contrasting color. A traditional feng shui solution would be to place bamboo flutes above (to symbolically raise the chi) alleviating any "weighty" effects. A faceted crystal prism hung over the bed will also help raise the chi.

Extremely lofty ceilings encourage the chi to move upward. If ceilings are too high, the chi will flow up and needs encouragement to come back down. Chi wants to fill the yang open space, so ceiling fans will do a nice job of keeping the chi circulating down to the lower levels. Whether fans are on and moving or not does not matter — the energy "gets the message."

Ceilings that are less than eight feet high tend to make us feel pushed down into the ground as if we are in a cave. This is a definite yin quality. Rooms with low ceilings need to be painted a light, warm color to offset and balance the energetic weight from above. Dark, yin colors will only emphasize the low ceilings and you will be stooping over before you know it.

Hallways — a Long Walk, Usually in the Dark

Especially in older homes, long hallways are often poorly lit, with bedrooms leading off to each side as you walk down what feels like a dark, boring tunnel. Modern home designs have shorter halls, yet the multiple doorway problem can remain. (See arguing and biting doors earlier in this chapter.)

To alleviate a long, dark tunnel effect, the best solution is a skylight or "solar tube" that will flood the passage with natural sunlight. Lighting a hallway makes the length appear shorter and gives an energetic lift to the space. This remedy is worth the cost, increases the real estate value, and owners will wonder why they did not do it years ago.

Faceted crystal prisms hung intermittently down a long hallway are a more typical feng shui solution and will help the chi slow down. They also add a pleasant visual diversion. Such treatments break up this rather boring area of the floor plan. My friend and feng shui colleague, Elliot Jay Tanzer, who has written the excellent book, *Choose the Best House for You; the Feng Shui Checklist,* recommends a runner carpet with a meandering pattern which adds warmth and slows down the speed of the sha chi. Also, pictures on the wall will create a diversion and act to slow down the flow of rushing chi.

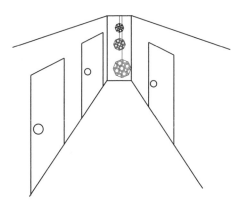

Chi rushing down a long hallway can be treated with faceted crystals. A skylight will also create less of a tunnel effect.

Pay It Forward — Precursor Energy

In feng shui, *precursor energy* refers to the energetic history of a property and whether it will affect you and your family in a positive way. As you already know, as part of their natal energy, houses have their own energy capacity which can be passed forward to new occupants. Make sure that previous owners have not been plagued with a string of serious misfortunes such as:

- divorce
- bankruptcy
- business failure
- chronic illness
- wayward children or early death of children
- general bad luck
- unnatural death in the house

Similar to an "energetic chain of title," (for readers familiar with real estate language) precursor energy from former inhabitants lingers in the house and keeps moving forward; this can seriously affect each new owner with the good or negative chi from the past. Naturally, you will find a few houses with some previous owner difficulties — but it should be a feng shui red flag if you discover a series of misfortunes to former occupants in the same property. The same goes for business locations.

In cases such as these, a professional "space clearing" or house blessing may go a long way toward alleviating the negative energetic implications for you and your family. It is also unlikely that former owners would have had the benefit of feng shui solutions, therefore using the space differently and applying feng shui techniques may alter the negative energy of a house. However, if the precursor energy is unusually strong and has plagued several previous owners in succession, you would be tempting fate to put yourself in energetic harm's way.

The only way to find out about such occurrences is to get a bit nosey. Yes, if you need to be a detective, so be it. Talking to neighbors and local store owners (especially in a smaller town) will yield much information. It is far better to know about previous owner problems before moving in than after moving in. Look on the bright side, maybe the earlier owners won the lottery! This benevolent and auspicious luck will also pay forward into your occupancy, so do your research and be a truly informed buyer.

You Have Only Just Begun

Congratulations! If you have read this book carefully, you are now ready to analyze real estate armed with new feng shui knowledge — and you may consider yourself an "enlightened" buyer or agent who has learned techniques many others are not aware of. You now have the edge of sharper scrutiny. The higher consciousness approach to selecting and purchasing real estate is now part of your thinking, and hopefully, your practice. As you use these feng shui techniques and suggestions while previewing houses for purchase, you will be assessing real estate much differently from when you first began reading this book. The *Feng Shui Property Appraisal*™ and the master Property Check List in the tear-out section will serve you well.

Keep in mind the many feng shui ideas you have learned and be selective using your newly trained feng shui eyes to analyze and choose your next home or investment. Above all, try not to be in a hurry or allow yourself to be rushed into a decision by others who are well-meaning, but who do not have the feng shui perspective that you do. This book was written to serve you in the best and highest way. Have fun, enjoy the process, and may the force of feng shui be with you!

Chapter 10 — Check Your *Chi* List

__ Is the front door in great shape (+) or does it need replacing or repainting? (-)

__ Is the front door in direct line with a back door or sliding door? (-)

__ Are there interior "arguing, biting, or contrary" doors? (-)

__ Are the windows in proportion to the doors? (+)

__ Can all windows open and are locks in good condition? (+)

__ Is there a staircase in front of the main door? (- -)

__ Does the house have a spiral staircase? (-) In the center of the house? (- -)

__ Do any stairways have open risers? (-)

__ Are there interior heavy beams or massive roof supports? (-)

__ Any interior posts or pillars? (-)

__ Are sloping ceilings over sitting or sleeping areas? (-)

__ Is there a long or dark hallway? (-)

__ Does the property have seriously negative "precursor" energy? (- -)

Special Supplement
Personal Directions and Flying Star Feng Shui

by Jami Lin

(Author's note: This Special Supplement is included for readers who want to know about astrological feng shui, learning Personal Directions, and determining the Flying Star energy for your new home. If you do not have an interest in these topics, that is fine; astrological feng shui is not for everyone. If you are interested in astrological feng shui, you will undoubtedly find the following information useful and fun to read. I also highly recommend receiving help from a well-trained feng shui consultant to help you interpret your Personal Directions and Flying Star feng shui.)

Using Natal and Personal Energies to Select Your New Home

I am thrilled that Holly has invited me to share some of the most exciting and powerful aspects of feng shui with you. Natal energies are the energies or the energetic conditions that are *already present* in a given space, such as location, lot shape, bagua layout in relation to floor plan, balance of yin and yang energy, presence of the Five Elements, etc.

If your home is located by a clear, flowing body of water, other nice homes, and lush green spaces, your property has better natal energy than if it is located next to a waste treatment plant. Based on your floor plan, natal energies are *how chi flows* throughout the house.

Natal energies are the energies of each bagua Life Aspiration (Wealth, Fame, Love and Romance, Children and Creativity, Helpful People, Career, Wisdom and Knowledge, and Family). As you learned in Chapter 5, the bagua energies also have an associated Element: Fire is the natal energy of the South, Water is the inherent energy of the North, Wood is at home in the East and Southeast, Earth is the natal energy of the Southwest and Northeast, and Metal dominates the energy of the West and Northwest.

When your house-to-be has good natal energy you can add personal decorative objects according to feng shui principles and the Five Elements to *enhance* your life potential. When your house-to-be has less favorable natal attributes, you can soften the negative energies with proper feng shui placement of furniture, use of color and decorative touches according to the Five Elements Holly has explained to you, etc. With positive possibilities from the start, life is so much more fun — you get to swim in the good flow, more joyfully and with greater ease!

When selecting a new house, you have two additional natal aspects that can lead to an even more beneficial outcome in your life. These two natal energies are based on time, and are often viewed as feng shui house astrology.

☯ The first Natal Energy is *specific to you* and is known as your *Personal Directions.* It is based on your date of birth.

☯ The second of these Natal Energies is *specific to your*

house and is called *Flying Star,* the ever-evolving time aspect in feng shui. Traditionally known as *San Yuan*, this system provides a consistent, yet ever-changing (flying) energetic influence based on the seasons and cycles of nature.

The General Premise of Natal Energies

A tree cannot live without its roots, trunk, and branches. Likewise, every feng shui item in your house is important; everything is holistically and energetically connected. If you love a house and it appears to be not-so-good from a feng shui perspective, use an experienced practitioner who will recommend one little energetic tweak or enhancement that will greatly improve the natal feng shui. Several tweaks can be even more helpful. If you see that your house-to-be has good feng shui, using Personal Directions and Flying Star feng shui can improve on the already good natal energy.

The key to "house-selecting feng shui," all the way to feng shui mastery, is analyzing and applying each aspect, or layer — chi flow, yin/yang, the bagua, the Five Elements, and site selection — to your potential property. Applying your Personal Directions and Flying Star information is like the frosting on the cake that emphasizes the best of all these aspects.

Part of masterful feng shui is about compromising to create as much good energy and harmony as possible. You may have a room with a negative feng shui poison arrow (such as a forceful inner corner) aiming at you while you sit at your desk. But, if the room has great Flying Stars and you can position your furniture so you sit facing one of your good Personal Directions and remedy the poison arrow, the room can be a winner!

The more you use feng shui, the better you will understand its many-layered aspects, and the more exciting feng shui becomes. For your house-purchasing quick evaluation, I provide you with basic Personal Direction and Flying Star charts later in this section. With these charts, almost at-a-glance, you can determine if the house is suitable or, better yet, a great choice!

Personal Directions Natal Energy

In Chinese, Personal Direction feng shui is called *Pa Chai*. The purpose of using the Personal Direction aspect of feng shui is just as its name suggests: to determine where your best energetic directions are located. You can use them to your advantage and receive optimum energy when sleeping, cooking, and sitting at your desk. We will start with finding your Personal Directions which are *based on your date of birth.* Here are Personal Direction basics:

- ☯ Each of us has four good and four not-so-good directions (the Yin and Yang energies — do you recognize the balance?).

- ☯ Because there are eight magnetic compass directions, there are eight different Personal Direction charts.

- ☯ Each chart is divided into eight directional areas (North, South, East, West, Northeast, Northwest, Southeast, and Southwest) plus the center sector. Does that remind you of the bagua?

- ☯ If a house is square or rectangular and has no missing areas, it has all eight-directional energies: four good and four not-so-good areas.

Which of the eight Personal Direction Charts works best for me?

Derived from the lo shu magic square (see page 35), "kua" numbers are the numbers found in this mathmatical construct from early feng shui history. Each Personal Direction chart is calculated from a feng shui or Kua number based on your birth year. *Men and women use different formulas to calculate their chart kua number.* There are two ways to easily determine your number.

- ☯ Do the math. (This is the fun way.)

- ☯ Use the Kua Number Chart following this explanation. (This is a good way to confirm that you did your math correctly.)

To do the math:

Men: Add the last two numbers from the year of your birth. If the last two digits of your birth year add up to a two-digit number (10 or more), add these two digits. That will reduce two digits to a single digit. Subtract your single digit answer from 10. The remainder is your Kua number. Select the chart with the same number (found in the center of each grid).

Example: Year of birth — 1965. 6+5 = 11 1+1 = 2. Subtract 2 from 10. Your answer is 8. You will use Kua Chart 8.

There are three exceptions:

1.) There is no #5 Kua Chart. If your answer is 5, use Kua Chart #2.

2.) If you were born on or before February 4th, use the previous year to make your calculations. (The 4th is correct except for the years when the Chinese New Year falls on the 5th! The solar new year falls on the 5th in: 1911, 1912, 1915, 1916, 1919, 1920, 1923, 1924, 1927, 1928, 1931, 1932, 1935, 1936, 1939, 1940, 1944, 1948, 1952, 1956, 1960, 1964, 1968, 1972, 1976, 1980, 2000, 2001, 2002, 2003, 2004.)

3.) For male children born after 2000, subtract the total of the last two digits of their birth years from 9 (instead of from 10).

Women: Add the last two numbers from the year of your birth. If the result is 10 or more, add the two digits together to reduce them to a single digit. Then add 5. If the result is 10 or more again, add these two digits (This will reduce them to a single number.) This single digit is your Kua number. Use that chart.

Example: Year of Birth — 1962. 6+2 = 8. Add 5 to 8 to get 13, another two-digit number. Add 1 to 3 to get your single-digit number (4). Use the Kua #4 Chart.

There are three exceptions:

1.) There is no #5 Kua Chart. If your answer is 5, use Kua Chart #8.

2.) If you were born on or before February 4th, use the previous year to make your calculations.

3.) For female children born after 2000 add 6 instead of 5.

If you have Internet access, point your browser to www.jamilin.com/free/direction.php to print your free, full-color, personalized chart.

Find Your Personal KUA Number
(line up your birth year)

											Male KUA	Female KUA
1918	1927	1936	1945	1954	1963	1972	1981	1990	1999	2008	1	8
1919	1929	1937	1946	1955	1964	1973	1982	1991	2000	2009	9	6
1920	1928	1938	1947	1956	1965	1974	1983	1992	2001	2010	8	7
1921	1930	1939	1948	1957	1966	1975	1984	1993	2002	2011	7	8
1922	1931	1940	1949	1958	1967	1976	1985	1994	2003	2012	6	9
1923	1932	1941	1950	1959	1968	1977	1986	1995	2004	2013	2	1
1924	1933	1942	1951	1960	1969	1978	1987	1996	2005	2014	4	2
1925	1934	1943	1952	1961	1970	1979	1988	1997	2006	2015	3	3
1926	1935	1944	1953	1962	1971	1980	1989	1998	2007	2016	2	4

If you were born between January 1 and February 4, use the year prior to your birth year. There is no KUA #5.

Record your kua number here for future reference: _____

You will now use this kua number to determine your Personal Directions. Knowing your Personal Directions will be valuable as you preview homes and use your Feng Shui Property Appraisal™ described in Chapter 6.

Got your Number? Select Your Chart!

Once you have determined your Kua number, you can determine whether you are an East House person or a West House person. (One house group is not better than the other; they are merely different directional energies.) Each of the charts below has a Kua number in the center to identify it. There are two sets of charts:

Kua Chart #s 1, 3, 4, and 9 are in the East House. East House favorable directional energies are in the North, South, East, and Southeast.

Kua Chart #s 2, 6, 7, and 8 are considered West House. West House favorable directional energies are in the West, Northwest, Northeast, and Southwest. Now, you can confirm your calculations by using the chart below.

EAST House

SE 1	S 3	SW 8
E 2	**1**	W 5
NE 6	N 4	NW 7

SE 3	S 1	SW 5
E 4	**3**	W 8
NE 7	N 2	NW 6

SE 4	S 2	SW 6
E 3	**4**	W 7
NE 8	N 1	NW 5

SE 2	S 4	SW 7
E 1	**9**	W 6
NE 5	N 3	NW 8

WEST House

SE 6	S 7	SW 4
E 5	**2**	W 2
NE 1	N 8	NW 3

SE 5	S 8	SW 3
E 6	**6**	W 1
NE 2	N 7	NW 4

SE 7	S 6	SW 2
E 8	**7**	W 4
NE 3	N 5	NW 1

SE 8	S 5	SW 1
E 7	**8**	W 3
NE 4	N 6	NW 2

Find your Kua number in the center of the appropriate grid.

The Kua numbers are the large numbers in the center of each grid. The smaller ones are the corresponding Personal Directions numbers.

☯ Tip!

All charts are oriented with South at the top according to traditional Chinese custom. Make sure you correctly align the compass points of the house with the compass directions of your Personal Direction chart.

In each directional area, there is a number 1 through 8. *These numbers indicate your Personal Directions* (#1 for Prosperity, Success, and Vitality) through to your really-not-so-good-direction (#8 for Disasters, Chronic Illness, and Bankruptcy) with the other numbers ranging in variable energies somewhere in between.

My four Positive Directions are: _____.

My four Not So Positive Directions are: _____.

The attributes of the Personal Numbers:

Positive
1 – Prosperity, Success, Vitality

2 – Health, Healing Energy, Good Fortune

3 – Longevity, Good Relations, Family Harmony

4 – Comfort, Stability, Harmony, Welcome

Not So Positive

5 – Difficulties, Quarrels, Frustrations

6 – Bad Luck, Income Loss

7 – Poor Health, Accidents, Litigations

8 – Disasters, Chronic Illness, Bankruptcy

Using the Personal Directions with a Floor Plan

Once you know your Kua number and your Personal Directions, it is simple to use your Kua number and Personal Directions with any floor plan. To take this next step, follow these directions which are a brief refresher from Holly's Chapter 6:

Take a compass reading from the "facing" direction of your house:

Standing outside the house at the front door (with your back flat against the door), hold the compass toward the direction straight out from the front door. Rotate the compass until the floating needle's red tip aligns with the "N." Keep the needle's red tip aligned with the letter "N." Continue to look straight ahead. The direction that is at the "top" of the compass (the farthest away from the house) is the direction you and your house are facing.

If the door is on an angle, or not on the same plane as the front of the house, place the back of your body against the front wall of the house to determine the "facing" direction. Be careful of any metal objects (including the door if it is metal) as metal may alter the compass reading.

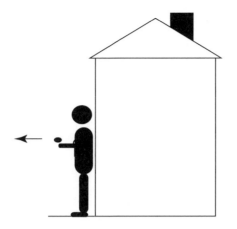

Take a compass reading with your back against the front door.

Sketch the Plan

Make sure you bring paper (graph paper available at office supplies store may be easier to use), a pencil, a ruler if you like, and an eraser. (See Holly's *Feng Shui Property Appraisal Kit* in Chapter 6.) Draw the outside shell of the house showing the relative lengths of various walls. Include any unusual exterior features such as angled walls or attached sunrooms.

Mark the main door's location. Generally the main door is the front door, which may sometimes be on the *side* of the house. Main doors on the side, or even the back, of the house may have better Personal Direction energies for you. You will see what I mean when you read the next section.

Continue to add details to your floor plan:

✓ Draw in the other doors leading to the outside.

✓ Add the major rooms to your drawing.

✓ Add the bedroom closets.

✓ Add the bathrooms and hallways.

Note: Do not worry if your plan is not perfectly to scale; you are probably not a professional draftsperson. However, be as detailed as possible; the more accurate your drawing the better you will be able to translate the chart information into *your* feng shui.

The Nine Bagua Life Aspirations

By now you are proficient in segmenting a house into nine equal bagua areas. (Refer to Chapter 2.) Remember, each area represents one of the eight directions with the tai chi being the ninth area (in the center).

Note: Because most houses are not perfect squares or rectangles, many rooms are not exactly defined by the nine equal areas of the bagua. You may have a missing area or a projection which you have already learned about in Chapter 8.

Quick tips:

- ☯ Any Life Aspiration (i.e., Wealth, Love and Romance) energy that occupies two-thirds or more of each room will determine the energy of the room.
- ☯ When two smaller rooms are located in one area, both rooms have the Life Aspiration energy of that area.
- ☯ When a large room is in multiple Life Aspirations, the energy of the room's main entrance takes precedence.

Enough prep, let's select your new home with good feng shui!

It is easy to spin the chart if the house faces a cardinal direction (N, S, E, W). *Important:* If your house faces East, orient your Personal Direction chart so the "E" aligns with the front door. If your house faces West, orient your Personal Direction chart so the "W" aligns with the front door, etc.

If the house has a non-cardinal direction (NE, SE, NW, SW), redraw the energies and do what I do to avoid making a mistake. Here is how to redraw the energies using the example of the Kua #7 chart overlaid on a Southwest facing chart.

N 5	NE 3	E 8
NW 1	**7**	7 SE
4 W	2 SW	6 S

#7 Kua Facing Southwest
Best Personal Directions are shaded gray.

This example is for a #7 Kua person with the house facing Southwest and the main door in the center of the front wall. Note that the best directions, 1, 2, 3, and 4 (shaded areas), are the same as if the house faced a true cardinal direction of N, S, E, or W. How wonderful to enter your house through your second Best Direction!

Using Your Best Personal Directions with a Floor Plan

You can use Best Personal Direction information in three powerful ways.

1. Location: Try to have your front door (or the main door you are going to use most of the time), and the doors to the master bedroom, kitchen, your home office (if you have one), and any room where you spend considerable time, in areas with good directional energies (areas 1-4).

Remember to compromise! Do not fret if portions of some important rooms are not located in one of your Best Direction locations; you have other options.

2. Facing Direction: Place the furniture where you spend considerable time so that you face one of your Best Personal Directions. While sitting or standing, you will want good energy coming toward the front of your body. While working in your kitchen, sitting at your computer or dining chair, reading, meditating, or even watching television, you want your chest to face one of your Best Directions.

"Facing" Direction When Sitting at Desk

When lying down, the top of your head becomes your "facing" direction. Sleep with the top of your head pointing toward one of your Best Directions. Easy! If you have health issues, face your #2 Best Direction, known as the "Doctor from Heaven" energy.

Facing Direction While Sleeping

3. Walk Through: When studying more advanced feng shui, you learn that the act of walking through your house activates chi. As you enter your house and walk through the most significant rooms, walk through your Best Facing Directions and Locations. By doing so, you "musk the room" (the same way a perfumed visitor leaves her scent trail) with your good directional chi.

My mate's Best Directions are different from mine. What can I do?
Remember the East and West House group difference? Do not panic if you and your loved one have different energies. My husband and I have "opposite House Group charts" yet after eighteen years, with good feng shui (and him being a saint), we are still going strong! There are good solutions.

If you and your partner are fortunate enough to be of the same house group, it is easy to feng shui your house with little compromise: your four Best Directions are the same as your partner's four best, just with different energetic qualities.

However, if you are like many couples, and one of you is an East House and the other a West House, then you will need to make some beneficial compromises. If the bedroom is already in one of his Best Locations, the bed can face one of her Best Directions.

Remember to look at the Best Locations and Best Directions of all household members. Reach harmonious compromises for each child too — one room may be better than another for each child's individual Best Directions.

Some rooms may be significantly better for home offices than others. Design your living arrangements so you spend most of your time in the rooms with your Best Directions. Arrange your kitchen so you can prepare and cook facing one of your good directions — you want to eat food that has been nourished and fed with good energy.

Your New Home's Flying Star Natal Energy

Now that you are understand your Personal Directions, we will move to the second natal energy: Flying Stars, the most profound and influential aspect of feng shui. *You will want to determine this important natal energy for any home on which you are considering making an offer.*

As Holly has explained, feng shui is based upon the natural laws and cycles of Mother Nature. As the days, weeks, and months flow into the seasons, the Earth is always changing, and so does your feng shui. Nothing is static. Everything is evolving, even us — and you surely will evolve during and after your move!

The ever-evolving time aspect in feng shui is called the Flying Stars. This system provides a consistent, yet ever-changing, energetic influence. The Flying Star cycles are of the same consistent natural science that we observe when the sun rises in the east, but, with the changing seasons, the compass degree where it rises appears differently on the horizon. Ever-changing, yet consistently predictable.

The Flying Stars can be described as the astrology of your house.

In the same way that the astrological alignment of the planets at the time you were born influences the natal character of your personality and destiny, the natal position of the "house stars" affect your good or not-so-great prosperity, success, relationships, and life condition.

The time that you move into your house determines your home's Flying Star energetic influence. Please note some feng shui masters disagree on what is the "right time" to determine the natal Flying Star house chart. They debate whether the energetic influence is determined by the year the house was built or the year that a person moves in.

> ***Assumption #1.*** One of the most fundamental feng shui rules is: *Activity* in an environment. If no one occupies a space, no one will experience its feng shui influence. If a house had been built 50 years ago and you moved in tomorrow, you bring your own energy into the space.

It is your chi that activates a space, making a house your home. This assumption rings true for me through my experience; how about you? Does the house feel differently than it did when you experienced it with the previous owner's furnishings or if it were empty? Do you feel the energetic change of a new beginning?

> ***Assumption #2.*** Because this book is being published in 2004 (a very exciting and auspicious time with its brand-new Period 8 cycle) and because you are considering buying a house now, simplified Period 8 charts are included toward the end of this Supplement so that you can buy your home smarter! The key is to select the house with the best natal Flying Star energies (and, of course, combine them with all the other good feng shui aspects you have already learned).

If you bought your home before 2004, you should still analyze the Flying Stars to enhance your feng shui as you will always benefit from this powerful energetic influence. I welcome you to contact me at JamiLin.com for charts for any previous years.

Here are the simplified Flying Star basics:

1. There are sixteen directional charts: two for each of the eight bagua directions: two for North, two for East, two for Northeast, etc.

2. Each of the sixteen charts has a different combination of energies *determined by the direction* a house is facing.

3. Each of the sixteen charts is segmented into eight bagua or directional areas with one in the center (sound familiar?). Each of the nine areas (including the center) has a unique natal Flying Star energy.

Which chart do I use?

Earlier in this section, you learned about Facing Direction and taking a compass reading. Now that you are a compass-reading pro, all you need to do is be a little more specific when taking your reading. There are two Flying Star charts for each of the eight directions: for example, the two North charts are called N1 and N2/3, the two Southeast charts are called SE1 and SE2/3, and so on.

Taking a compass reading is just as easy as it was before. While standing outside with your back to the main door, instead of just reading the compass direction, *determine (as carefully as you can) the number of the compass degree* (for example, 127 degrees). Then determine which of the sixteen directional charts you will need to use by referencing the chart on the following page.

Directional Degree	Chart	Directional Degree	Chart
337.5 to 352.5	N 1	157.5 to 172.5	S 1
352.5 to 22.5	N 2/3	172.5 to 202.5	S 2/3
22.5 to 37.5	NE 1	202.5 to 217.5	SW 1
37.5 to 67.5	NE 2/3	217.5 to 247.5	SW 2/3
67.5 to 82.5	E 1	247.5 to 262.5	W 1
82.5 to 112.5	E 2/3	262.5 to 292.5	W 2/3
112.5 to 127.5	SE 1	292.5 to 307.5	NW 1
127.5 to 157.5	SE 2/3	307.5 to 337.5	NW 2/3

Standard Heading (Degree) to Chart Index

To make it easy for you to analyze the energy of your house-to-be, the charts are oriented in the direction that the house is facing. For example, if a house is facing between 172.5 to 202.5 degrees, the S 2/3 is the correct chart. (All sixteen directional Flying Star charts are located at the end of this section.)

Example using S 2/3 chart:

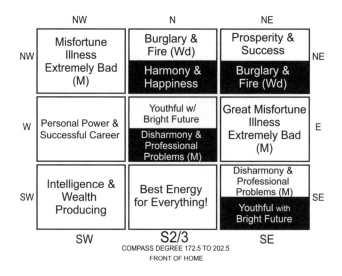

For clarification, the front door, based on the floor plan, may be in one of these locations:

Left, where you enter through the SW area and musk the house with *Intelligence & Wealth-Producing Talent, Authority* energy.

Center, (the more architecturally standard location) where you enter through the S area and musk the house with *Spiritual & Honorable, Longevity with Financial Success: the best energy of Period 8!*

Right, where if your door is in the SE area, you will notice two energies present and you need to determine which one to use based upon if the room is yin or yang. If the room is yin, the energy is youthful with a bright future. If the room is yang, you will receive energy in that space along with its "walk through" benefits, disharmony and professional problems.

The Flying Stars—Yin and Yang Aspects

As you remember in Chapter 3, Holly provided detail on the importance of yin and yang energies. Now, it is easy to put your yin and yang knowledge to work with your Flying Stars.

- ☯ If a room is *active*, such as an entry, kitchen, living, dining, family, playroom, or your home office, it is a *yang* area and you use the yang energetic attribute. ***Note: Yang energies are indicated in the charts by standard black text.***

- ☯ If a room is *quiet*, such as a bedroom or meditation room, it is a *yin* area and you use the yin energetic attribute. ***Note: Yin energies are indicated in the charts by white text on a black background.***

In each of the sixteen charts, you will notice that some of the areas have just one energetic description while others have two. If there is just one description, the energy is the same for either a yin or yang room. ***Note:*** **When the energy is either yin or yang, the text is in standard black.**

In the S 2/3 chart, here are where the best energetic rooms are located:

Location	Yin / Quiet Room	Yang/Active Room
N	good	not favorable
NE	not favorable	good
E	not favorable	not favorable
SE	good	not favorable
S	good	good
SW	good	good
W	good	good
NW	not favorable	not favorable

Important note: No house has perfect feng shui. The objective is not unreachable perfection; it is to create yin and yang balance by activating and enhancing the good energies while reducing the not-so-good energies.

Combining Flying Stars with your Best Personal Directions

If a home's Flying Star energies are located in the same areas as your Best Directions, oo-la-la! *The location objective* is to have as many good Flying Star locations and Best Personal Directions as possible, especially in the most significant rooms (master bedroom, kitchen, office, living room).

Using exactly the same layout and furniture placement concepts as in the Personal Direction section, you can "sit" with your chest facing, and sleep with the top of your head pointing toward the direction of good

Flying Stars. Example, using the S 2/3 chart: Let us say that you need a home office, and of course, a place to sleep.

First prioritize location:

The yin bedroom should be North for Life Harmony and Happiness energy. The yang home office should be in the Northeast for Prosperity and Success

Then prioritize furniture directions:

In the North yin bedroom, position your head to point toward directions with good Flying Stars: N, S, SW, or W. Compromise with the layout of the room for good Personal Direction (It is best to sleep facing N or S if you are an East Group person and W or SW if you are a West Group person.)

In the Northeast yang office, position your desk so that your chest faces good Flying Stars as you sit: NE, S, SW, or W. Again, consider the architectural layout of the room and which is a good Personal Direction. (If you are an East group person, it is best to sit with your chest facing S or SE and if you are from the West Group, it is best to sit facing SW or W.) But because no house is perfect, what happens if you have to use a room with not-so-good location energy?

Direction is much more important than location.

In other words, receiving energy from good Flying Star directions and your Best Personal Directions (through your chest or the top of your head) is more valuable than sitting or sleeping in your Best Personal Direction. However, if you must occupy a room with less-favorable Flying Stars, sit and/or sleep in one of your Best Directions.

Improving your Personal Direction and Flying Star Feng Shui!

Because you already know there is no house with perfect feng shui, included in the Flying Star charts are letters in parenthesis to help you reduce unfavorable energies. With the help of a qualified feng shui practitioner, when you decorate and add some M (Metal), W (Water), or Wd (Wood) Element, you will reduce some of the negative energy with the mitigating (balancing) Element.

To buy your home smarter, I cannot stress enough that the better the natal energies, Flying Stars, and Best Personal Directions are from the start, the better and more gracious your life will be. When you enhance the good "raw materials" with all the other feng shui attributes of color, texture, furniture, accessories, and art with your own decorating style, *your feng shui and life potential will be that much greater*.

On the following pages are the sixteen Flying Star charts for each of the directions a house might face.

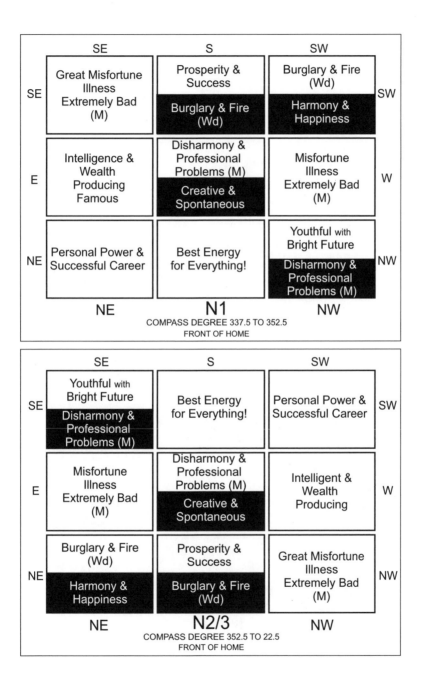

	SE	S	SW	
SE	Great Misfortune Illness Extremely Bad (M)	Prosperity & Success / Burglary & Fire (Wd)	Burglary & Fire (Wd) / Harmony & Happiness	SW
E	Intelligence & Wealth Producing Famous	Disharmony & Professional Problems (M) / Creative & Spontaneous	Misfortune Illness Extremely Bad (M)	W
NE	Personal Power & Successful Career	Best Energy for Everything!	Youthful with Bright Future / Disharmony & Professional Problems (M)	NW
	NE	N1	NW	

COMPASS DEGREE 337.5 TO 352.5
FRONT OF HOME

	SE	S	SW	
SE	Youthful with Bright Future / Disharmony & Professional Problems (M)	Best Energy for Everything!	Personal Power & Successful Career	SW
E	Misfortune Illness Extremely Bad (M)	Disharmony & Professional Problems (M) / Creative & Spontaneous	Intelligent & Wealth Producing	W
NE	Burglary & Fire (Wd) / Harmony & Happiness	Prosperity & Success / Burglary & Fire (Wd)	Great Misfortune Illness Extremely Bad (M)	NW
	NE	N2/3	NW	

COMPASS DEGREE 352.5 TO 22.5
FRONT OF HOME

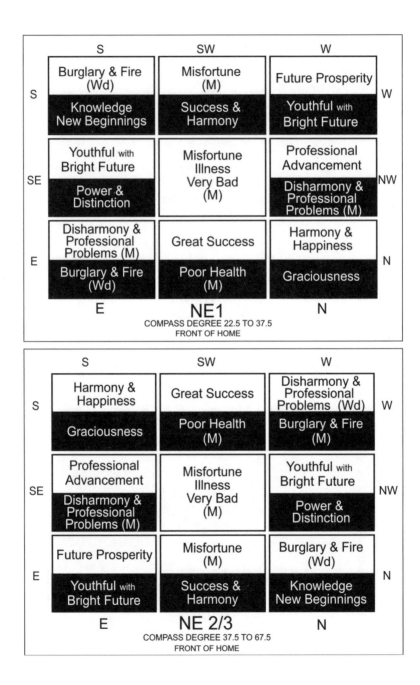

NE1
COMPASS DEGREE 22.5 TO 37.5
FRONT OF HOME

NE 2/3
COMPASS DEGREE 37.5 TO 67.5
FRONT OF HOME

248

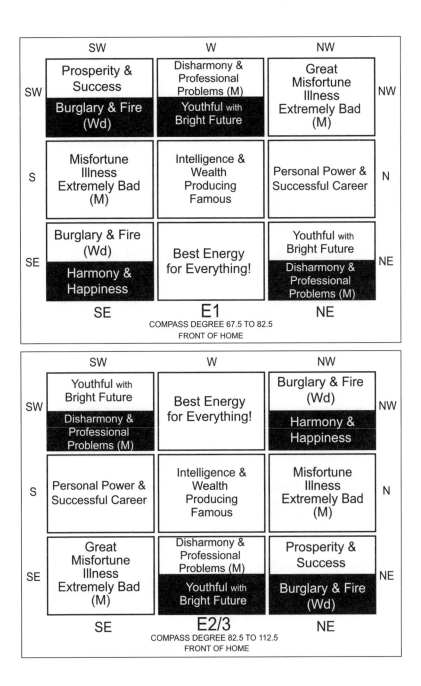

	SW	W	NW	
SW	Prosperity & Success / **Burglary & Fire (Wd)**	Disharmony & Professional Problems (M) / **Youthful with Bright Future**	Great Misfortune Illness Extremely Bad (M)	**NW**
S	Misfortune Illness Extremely Bad (M)	Intelligence & Wealth Producing Famous	Personal Power & Successful Career	**N**
SE	Burglary & Fire (Wd) / **Harmony & Happiness**	Best Energy for Everything!	Youthful with Bright Future / **Disharmony & Professional Problems (M)**	**NE**
	SE	E1	NE	

COMPASS DEGREE 67.5 TO 82.5
FRONT OF HOME

	SW	W	NW	
SW	Youthful with Bright Future / **Disharmony & Professional Problems (M)**	Best Energy for Everything!	Burglary & Fire (Wd) / **Harmony & Happiness**	**NW**
S	Personal Power & Successful Career	Intelligence & Wealth Producing Famous	Misfortune Illness Extremely Bad (M)	**N**
SE	Great Misfortune Illness Extremely Bad (M)	Disharmony & Professional Problems (M) / **Youthful with Bright Future**	Prosperity & Success / **Burglary & Fire (Wd)**	**NE**
	SE	E2/3	NE	

COMPASS DEGREE 82.5 TO 112.5
FRONT OF HOME

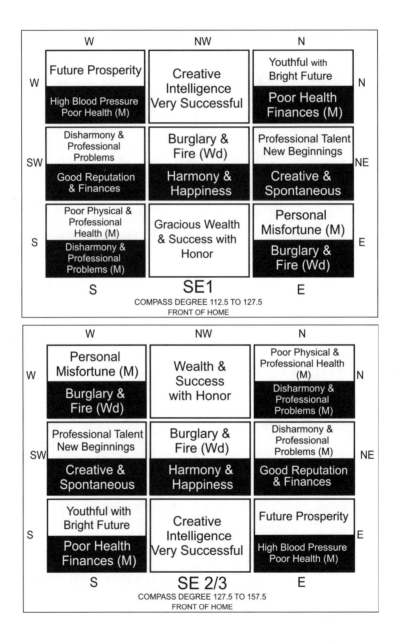

SE1
COMPASS DEGREE 112.5 TO 127.5
FRONT OF HOME

SE 2/3
COMPASS DEGREE 127.5 TO 157.5
FRONT OF HOME

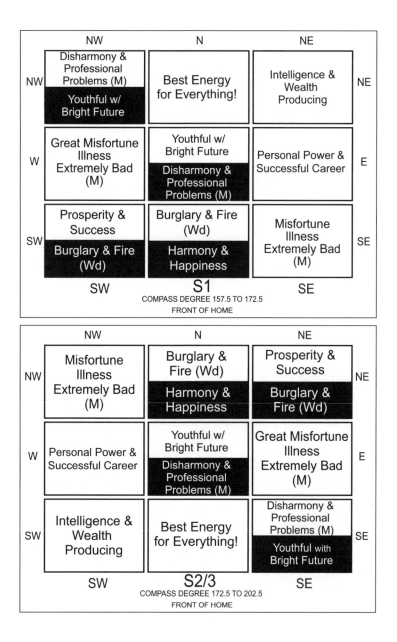

S1

COMPASS DEGREE 157.5 TO 172.5

FRONT OF HOME

S2/3

COMPASS DEGREE 172.5 TO 202.5

FRONT OF HOME

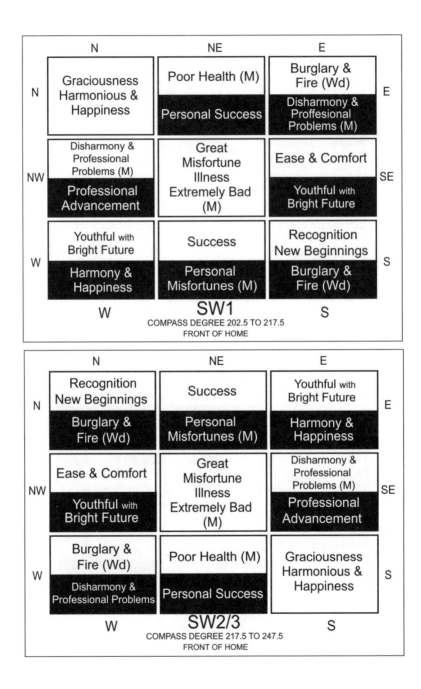

SW1
COMPASS DEGREE 202.5 TO 217.5
FRONT OF HOME

SW2/3
COMPASS DEGREE 217.5 TO 247.5
FRONT OF HOME

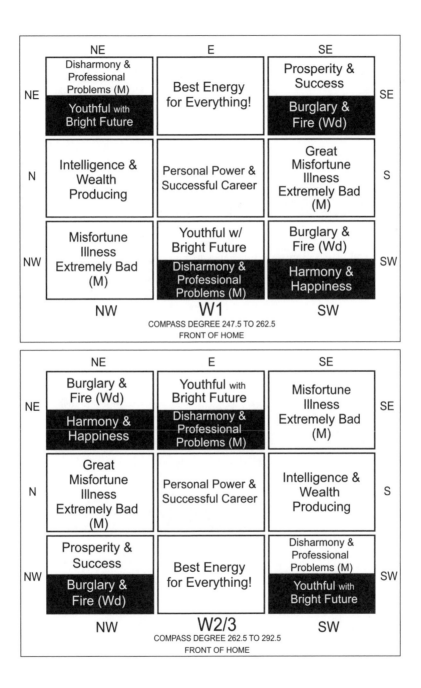

W1

COMPASS DEGREE 247.5 TO 262.5
FRONT OF HOME

W2/3

COMPASS DEGREE 262.5 TO 292.5
FRONT OF HOME

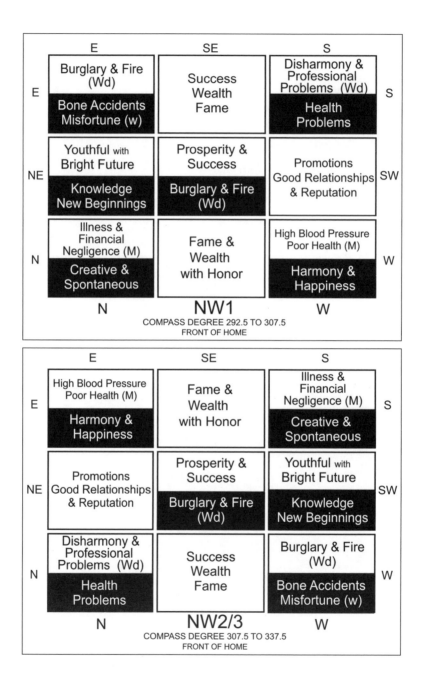

NW1
COMPASS DEGREE 292.5 TO 307.5
FRONT OF HOME

NW2/3
COMPASS DEGREE 307.5 TO 337.5
FRONT OF HOME

254

Why is this aspect of Feng Shui called the Flying Stars?

Now that you have had your basic Flying Star lesson, you might think it is silly to discuss why this system is called the Flying Stars. I would be remiss in my feng shui explanation if I did not tell you that as Flying Stars change (fly) every twenty years (remember we are now in Period 8), energy also cycles every year, month, and day, each with a unique energetic influence. Similarly, as each year, month, and day provides you with different experiences — some good, some not-so-good, there are unique Flying Star energies, some good, and conversely, some not-so-good. I am sure a professional feng shui consultant, knowledgeable in this Compass School approach, can assist you in tapping into these.

The most important tip you need! If there were only one consideration to make once you think you have found the right house, in the perfect location with the floor plan that meets your needs, it would be to check your natal feng shui of Personal Directions and Flying Stars, *before* you put your money down!

With good natal feng shui, once the house is your new home, by adding your cosmetic feng shui (furniture, art and accessory placement, color and textures of floors, walls, and fabrics along with your personalized, Elemental enhancements), your home will truly be of beneficial service to you and not just a place to live. Love your home and have your home love you!

Jami Lin frequently speaks at conferences around the globe and her best-selling feng shui books are internationally acclaimed. Sharing her knowledge and expertise world-wide, Jami Lin integrates the most effective feng shui techniques from the entire scope of traditions and invites you to master them too. These include Flying Star, Eight Mansions, Compass and Black Hat Sect along with humanitarian, psychological, healing, and intuition for empowering home, office, and garden feng shui. She adds creative design, her loving heart and deep spiritual sensitivity.

Visit www.jamilin.com *or call 305.893.9985 for the most effective and powerful feng shui advice. Her great website offers free and expert daily tips, inspirations, newsletter, decorative products and Home-Study Mastery classes.*

Appendix A
Your Celestial Animal, Kua Numbers, and Personal Element

The following chart will show you the Kua Numbers you need to determine your Personal Directions. *If your birth date is on or between January 1st and February 4th, use the year prior to your actual birth year.* However, if your birth year is preceded by an asterisk (*) and you were born on February 5th, use the prior year. Although celestial animal signs do not pertain to purchasing real estate, I include them here because they are of interest to many feng shui devotees. Your Kua number will help determine your Personal Directions (see Special Supplement).

	Birth Year	Celestial Animal	Male Kua	Personal Element	Female Kua	Personal Element
	1925	Ox	9	Fire	6	Metal
	1926	Tiger	8	Earth	7	Metal
*	1927	Rabbit	7	Metal	8	Earth
*	1928	Dragon	6	Metal	9	Fire
	1929	Snake	2	Earth	1	Water
	1930	Horse	4	Wood	2	Earth
*	1931	Goat	3	Wood	3	Wood
*	1932	Monkey	2	Earth	4	Wood

	Birth Year	Celestial Animal	Male Kua	Personal Elemant	Female Kua	Personal Element
	1933	Rooster	1	Water	8	Earth
	1934	Dog	9	Fire	6	Metal
*	1935	Boar	2	Earth	4	Wood
*	1936	Rat	1	Water	8	Earth
	1937	Ox	9	Fire	6	Metal
	1938	Tiger	8	Earth	7	Metal
*	1939	Rabbit	7	Metal	8	Earth
*	1940	Dragon	6	Metal	9	Fire
	1941	Snake	2	Earth	1	Water
	1942	Horse	4	Wood	2	Earth
	1943	Goat	3	Wood	3	Wood
*	1944	Monkey	2	Earth	4	Wood
	1945	Rooster	1	Water	8	Earth
	1946	Dog	9	Fire	6	Metal
	1947	Boar	8	Earth	7	Metal
*	1948	Rat	7	Metal	8	Earth
	1949	Ox	6	Metal	9	Fire
	1950	Tiger	3	Earth	1	Water
	1951	Rabbit	4	Wood	2	Earth
*	1952	Dragon	2	Wood	3	Wood
	1953	Snake	2	Earth	4	Wood
	1954	Horse	1	Water	8	Earth
	1955	Goat	9	Fire	6	Metal
*	1956	Monkey	8	Earth	7	Metal
	1957	Rooster	7	Metal	8	Earth
	1958	Dog	6	Metal	9	Fire
	1959	Boar	2	Earth	1	Water
*	1960	Rat	4	Wood	2	Earth
	1961	Ox	3	Wood	3	Wood
	1962	Tiger	2	Earth	4	Wood

	Birth Year	Celestial Animal	Male Kua	Personal Element	Female Kua	Personal Element
	1963	Rabbit	1	Water	8	Earth
*	1964	Dragon	9	Fire	6	Metal
	1965	Snake	8	Earth	7	Metal
	1966	Horse	7	Metal	8	Earth
	1967	Goat	6	Metal	9	Fire
*	1968	Monkey	2	Earth	1	Water
	1969	Rooster	4	Wood	2	Earth
	1970	Dog	3	Wood	3	Wood
	1971	Boar	2	Earth	4	Wood
*	1972	Rat	1	Water	8	Earth
	1973	Ox	9	Fire	6	Metal
	1974	Tiger	8	Earth	7	Metal
	1975	Rabbit	7	Metal	8	Earth
*	1976	Dragon	6	Metal	9	Fire
	1977	Snake	2	Earth	1	Water
	1978	Horse	4	Wood	2	Earth
	1979	Goat	3	Wood	3	Wood
*	1980	Monkey	2	Earth	4	Wood
	1981	Rooster	1	Water	8	Earth
	1982	Dog	9	Fire	6	Metal
	1983	Boar	8	Earth	7	Metal
	1984	Rat	7	Metal	8	Earth
	1985	Ox	6	Metal	9	Fire
	1986	Tiger	2	Earth	1	Water
	1987	Rabbit	4	Wood	2	Earth
	1988	Dragon	3	Wood	3	Wood
	1989	Snake	2	Earth	4	Wood
	1990	Horse	1	Water	8	Earth
	1991	Goat	9	Fire	6	Metal
	1992	Monkey	8	Earth	7	Metal

	Birth Year	Celestial Animal	Male Kua	Personal Element	Female Kua	Personal Element
	1993	Rooster	7	Metal	8	Earth
	1994	Dog	6	Metal	9	Fire
	1995	Boar	2	Earth	1	Water
	1996	Rat	4	Wood	2	Earth
	1997	Ox	3	Wood	3	Wood
	1998	Tiger	2	Earth	4	Wood
	1999	Rabbit	1	Water	8	Earth
*	2000	Dragon	9	Fire	6	Metal
*	2001	Snake	8	Earth	7	Metal
	2002	Horse	7	Metal	8	Earth
*	2003	Goat	6	Metal	9	Fire
*	2004	Monkey	2	Earth	1	Water
	2005	Rooster	4	Wood	2	Earth
	2006	Dog	3	Wood	3	Wood
	2007	Boar	2	Earth	4	Wood
	2008	Rat	1	Water	8	Earth
	2009	Ox	8	Earth	7	Metal
	2010	Tiger	6	Metal	9	Fire

260

Appendix B
Feng Shui Significance of Colors and Numbers

Colors

As Professor Lin Yun said, "...color defines for us what exists and what does not exist. (It) discloses the status of one's health... inspires emotion... and structures our behavior." [6] Color affects our moods and alters our perception of space within an environment. In feng shui, color plays a significant role in the implementation of solutions to challenges both in interior design and outside the home in landscaping. Color is tied to the cycles of the Five Elements, and each Element has its associated hue.

Red: *Fire Element*, happiness, power, luck, passion, fame, aggression, summer.

Yellow: *Earth Element*, stability, royalty, gaiety, patience, wisdom, autumn.

Orange: *Fire or Earth*, happiness, power, autumn.

Green: *Wood Element*, growth, inspiration, rebirth, eternity, harmony, spring.

Blue: *Water Element*, heaven, clarity of purpose.

Purple: *(No Element)* high office, wealth, power, spirituality

Gray: *Metal Element*, ambivalence, frustration,

---

[6] *Living Color*, Grand Master Lin Yun & Sarah Rossbach, p.11.

ambiguity, hopelessness.

White: *Metal Element*, purity, precision, rigidity. (In China used for mourning. In the West it also is used as a shroud and is ghostlike.)

Black: *Water Element*, spirituality, intellectual depth, wisdom, winter.

Brown: *Earth Element*, stability, depth, endurance, autumn.

Gold: *Metal Element*, wealth, power.

Numbers

Numbers are highly significant in feng shui, and in China numbers play an important role in the selection of addresses, choosing license plates, and determining dates for significant events such as a marriage or the opening of a business. When spoken, numbers sound like other words. Numbers that sound similar to fortunate, positive words are considered lucky numbers. Numbers that sound like things that are bad (death, poverty) are considered unlucky. Even numbers are yin and odd numbers are yang.

In general, yang numbers are considered more fortunate than those that are yin. In Chinese the number four sounds similar to the word "death." In Chinese hotels, it is not unusual to omit the designation of the fourth floor, while in the West, often naming the thirteenth floor is omitted.) When considering an address, numbers are added together until the final result is less than 10.

For example - 2874 Easy Street would be figured as follows:

$$2 + 8 = 10 \qquad +7 = 17 \qquad +4 = 21 \qquad 2 + 1 = 3$$

Zero: represents perfection, completion, and harmony.

One: in Chinese, the word for one sounds like the word for honor… considered lucky; represents the Water Element and the direction North.

Two: sounds similar to the word for sure. Two stands for *doubling up* as in *multiplying your happiness* and is considered a good number. It corresponds with Earth and Southwest.

Three: sounds like the word for growth, or alive, and is considered lucky; represents Wood and East.

Four: very similar to the word for death and felt to be very unlucky unless combined with a favorable number such as 48. Four represents the Southeast direction and the Wood Element.

Five: represents the central bagua position on the Lo-Shu Magic Square and signifies balance.

Six: sounds like the word for *wealth*, making it very popular. Represents the Metal Element and the direction West.

Seven: also sounds like the word for *sure*, and is considered to be a very fortunate number; represents Metal and Northwest.

Eight: similar to the word *multiply* and is extremely lucky; considered to be a fertile number, so if you desire many children, live in a house with this address; represents the Earth Element and Southeast.

Nine: considered to be one of the luckiest numbers because it sounds like the word for longevity and long life; is the highest of the single digit, whole numbers; represents the Fire Element and the South.

Note: The above associations with numbers are based on Chinese cultural symbology developed over countless generations and are presented here for those interested. Western associations with numbers have different implications.

Appendix C
Feng Shui Enhancements and Solutions

Feng shui enhancements are intended to alter chi, for the better of course! There are many such adjustments, ranging from the very simple to the rather complicated. They can be divided into categories by the *effect they are designed to achieve.*

Part of the fun of feng shui is to experiment with enhancements, keeping in mind the result you want. Make sure that as you position your solution or enhancement you set a strong mental intention that will constantly remind you what alteration of chi you wish to accomplish.

For example, if you are absolutely in love with a house, yet you know from reading this book there is a powerful high tension electric transformer aiming at your house from across the street, the use of a bagua mirror, always hung outside, and centered above your front door would be an appropriate treatment for the sha arrow, but not the electromagnetic frequencies.

As you hang the bagua mirror set a firm intention — that the negative sha chi from the power transformer is deflected away from your property. Keep in mind that this solution does not prevent the electromagnetic frequencies from continually bombarding the property; I would strongly advise against purchasing a home near a powerful electric transformer.

Effect on Chi	Solution
Disperse or slow down	faceted prism crystal
Soften	fountain, plants, gently draped fabric
Deflect	faceted prism crystal, reflective surface
Block or stop (as in sha chi)	bagua mirror, reflective surface
Make energetically disappear	mirror as much surface as possible
Lift or raise	bamboo flutes, mirror, lights, wind chimes, fountain, flags/whirligigs, candles, music, incense, plants
Multiply	mirror (larger the better)
Strengthen	boulder, trees, large shrubs,
Ground (solidify)	plants, rocks, boulders, trees, statues

The transcendental Black Sect treatment for a bathroom in the center of a house is to mirror the interior, thus making the offensive room "disappear." A mirror on the outside of the bathroom door deflects the chi away. A mundane treatment would be to paint the bathroom in earth tones and use earth tone towels. Also make use of tiles (Earth Elements) which elementally "absorb" the Water Element. A plant on top of the toilet tank will also help. (*Note:* Also be aware that chi is affected by the use and balancing of the Five Elements. See Chapter 5.)

Be careful in your use of mirrors as feng shui solutions. You do not want to create a fragmented or distorted appearance, such as placing a mirror in such a way that the head, or a portion of the face is not visible. It may seem like a contradiction, but besides making things disappear, mirrors also *multiply* what they reflect, whether it is positive or negative. Reflecting a great view is lovely; reflecting (multiplying) a sha arrow such as an electric transformer is not what you want to do.

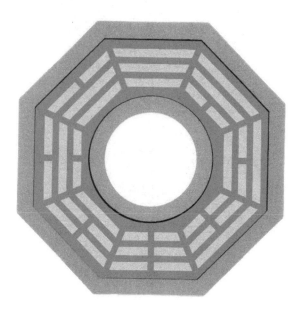

Bagua Mirror

Glossary of Real Estate Terms

agency　　　　term used to indicate the type of professional, fiduciary relationship that exists between buyers and sellers and their respective real estate agents.

close of escrow　　day on which the property is recorded at the county recorder's office in the new buyers' names and becomes part of public record. This is your goal!

closing costs　　various fees associated with closing the escrow. Buyer and seller each have their respective costs including, but not limited to, title search, loan transfer, recording, and hazard disclosure searches.

CMA　　　　competitive market analysis, performed by a real estate agent showing what price would be most appropriate for any given home in the current market based on sales of similar homes during the previous six months.

contingency　　serious condition imposed upon a contract, usually by buyers, which, if not fulfilled or waived, can cause the contract to cancel.

commission　　a negotiable fee paid to a real estate broker (then to an agent) for services performed in the buying or selling of real estate. Paid from sellers' proceeds at close of escrow.

counter offer   offer subsequent to an original offer to purchase. There may be more than one counter offer.

curb appeal   condition of a property as seen from the street. Usually has *significant* impact on a prospective buyers' impressions either for better or worse.

disclosure   responsibility of sellers to state in writing anything of a material nature they are aware of regarding the property they are selling. The responsibility for complete disclosure also falls on the agent representing the sellers.

discovery period   time limit buyers have to complete all their investigations regarding property they are buying. This time limit is stated in the contract and binds all parties.

equity   value of a property over and above the mortgage and other liabilities (including closing costs) relating to it.

earnest money deposit   sum deposited by buyer when submitting an offer to purchase real estate.

escrow company   neutral third party that assists buyers and sellers with necessary documentation in the process of selling/buying real estate.

escrow fees   technically, only the costs paid to the escrow company for their services; usually paid in equal amounts by the buyer and seller at close of escrow. Sometimes "escrow fees" is used to refer to *all* the costs in connection with closing an escrow.

escrow instructions	documentation of the purchase contract agreed to between buyer and seller.
fiduciary	legal relationship of loyalty that exists between an agent and his principal (a buyer or seller).
final walk through	prior to close of escrow, the buyer and the buyer's agent have a final inspection of the property. This usually takes place during the last week of escrow.
FSBO	*(pronounced fizz-bow)* For Sale by Owner.
gift down payment	portion of the cash down payment coming from the buyers which has been *gifted* to them from a third party. A lender will usually require a written explanation from the giver that this money does not have to be repaid.
grant deed	legal document signed by the seller passing ownership to the new buyer; should be recorded.
home inspection	thorough inspection to discover and disclose the structural and mechanical condition of a structure to the buyer, the results of which are in written report form. Should be performed by a professional home inspector. Can be ordered by either a buyer or seller.
home warranty	one year insurance plan providing coverage for a majority of the mechanical aspects of a property.
lender	bank, savings and loan, mortgage

banker, or mortgage broker who lends the buyer funds to purchase property.

lien
(*pronounced lean*) monetary amount recorded against a property. This could be the result of a bill left unpaid or a disagreement with a contractor. Escrow cannot close until liens are paid or cleared from title.

listing
written agreement between a seller and a listing real estate broker authorizing the broker to offer the property for sale on behalf of the seller.

lock box
device, provided by a real estate agent, holding a key to the premises in a secure manner, allowing only authorized persons to enter.

MLS
abbreviation for *Multiple Listing Service*. Local real estate organization that provides detailed information to member brokers and agents, in book format and by on-line data base.

mortgage
usually refers to the loan obtained by the buyer and secured by a piece of real estate. In most states mortgages are secured by a Note and Deed of Trust.

mortgage banker
a lender in control of the final funding; the mortgage banker is *the bank* and needs no underwriting from outside sources. (*Note:* mortgage *broker* and a mortgage *banker* are not the same thing. *See next listing.*)

mortgage broker
broker that works with many different lending institutions, similar to an

insurance broker, who places a loan with the best available source. *The broker is not in control of final funding*, but rather acts as a middleman to place a loan on behalf of the buyer client.

real estate agent individual licensed to practice and derive compensation for the buying and selling of real estate; must have their license listed under a real estate *broker*.

real estate broker individual who has passed a broker examination; an employer of real estate agents. Bears legal and professional responsibility for the actions of agents who work under the broker's license.

REALTOR® designation given to members of the National Association of REALTORS®, which holds its members to a strict professional code of ethics in assisting buyers and sellers with real estate. (*Note:* not all real estate agents and brokers are REALTORS®.)

red flag condition of the property that warns a buyer or agent that a problem exists; for example, serious erosion, cracked foundation, or un-level flooring.

title manner in which real estate is legally held and recorded. It is very important to be clear about how title to property is taken; can have serious tax and estate consequences.

twin home sometimes called a "zero-lot-line-home"; has a common wall down the center with each side having separate ownership.

Glossary of Feng Shui Terms

arguing doors
doors which are awkwardly placed and when opened, bump into each other.

bagua
ancient eight-sided energy template used in feng shui for mapping of the eight Life Areas.

bagua mirror
octagonal shaped device with a circular central mirror, always hung on the outside of a building and usually centered over the front door to ward off sha chi coming from an external force such as a tall building or nearby freeway traffic.

bau-biologie
translated from German as "building of living things," a current movement that encourages the holistic, healing home. First developed in Germany, bau-biologie has a strong environmental emphasis applied to both structures and the materials within buildings.

biting doors
doors which are unevenly aligned, as in a hallway or corridor.

Black Sect School
brought to the West by H.H. Grand Master Prof. Thomas Lin Yun in the 1980s from China. BTB emphasizes transcendental or mystical cures. The setting of intention is considered to be the prime factor that activates beneficial chi. BTB combines Tibetan tantric traditions, and is extremely popular in the United States.

Book of Changes
also known as the *I Ching*, considered to be the oldest book of Chinese wisdom emphasizing *right conduct of the superior man*. Still in

widespread use today as a guide and an oracle.

chi *(pronounced chee)* the cosmic breath of life; the energy which flows throughout the universe and permeates the land, people, and spaces within buildings giving the "life force" to all things.

Chinese New Year usually falls close to the first week in February on the Western calendar, and is named in cycles for the twelve celestial animals of the zodiac: Rat, Ox, Tiger, Hare, Dragon, Snake, Horse, Sheep, Monkey, Cock, Dog, Boar.

command position the area in a room, farthest from the doorway, yet facing the door; a bed, desk chair, or any seating placed in this position provides the utmost visibility and security. Also referred to as the "power position."

Compass School (also called the *Fukien School),* school that applies feng shui principles according to directional orientation and relies on the use of the feng shui compass, or luo-pan. Compass School feng shui lays stress on the eight trigrams of the *I Ching*, the Heavenly Stems, the Earthly Branches, and the Constellations. Originated approximately 960 A.D.

Controlling Cycle of Elements
used in both interior and exterior design. This cycle of elements acts to "balance or control" one another. Metal cuts wood, wood displaces earth, earth dams water, water extinguishes fire, fire burns wood.

crystals considered in feng shui to be strong earth energy enhancers, diffusers, and deflectors of sha chi. Both natural and man-made crystals are effective and are used for different purposes.

dragon lines	a Chinese geomancer's description of pathways of energetic power very similar to the ley lines described by Alfred Watkins, a British scientist and photographer.
Earthly Branches	the twelve Earthly Branches give specific information about time and place on the feng shui compass. Associated with location of earth (dragon) chi, they also indicate the twelve double-hour divisions of the day, as well as the twelve months of the year. (Skinner, p.79)
feng shui	*(pronounced fung schway)* translated from the Chinese means wind and water. The ancient art/ design science of harmony and balance within an environment.
Five Elements	fire, earth, metal, water, and wood, which, according to ancient Chinese tradition, comprises all life on earth (called *wu-hsing* in Chinese).
Form School	the original school of feng shui which developed in the south of China over three thousand years ago.
geomancy	a former term for feng shui, inappropriately used today. More correctly, geomancy relates to an Arab form of divination. (Skinner, p. xi)
hexagrams	the sixty-four combinations of trigrams from the *I Ching.*
I Ching	*(pronounced ee ching)* also called *The Book of Changes*; said to be the oldest source of Chinese right conduct, containing the sixty-four hexagrams on which, among other things, feng shui is based.
intention, setting of	
	the most powerful and important aspect of

deriving benefits from feng shui, and especially emphasized in the Black Tibetan Sect School.

intuitive school not a specific *school* as such, intuitive feng shui is practiced instinctively by artists, interior designers, architects, and lay persons with natural artistic talent.

Kan-yu (*pronounced kan-yoo*) term for early form of feng shui.

Later Heaven sequence

arrangement of the bagua trigrams to better suit the "homes of the living" as opposed to the "homes of the dead" or graves in early feng shui practice.

ley lines term coined by Alfred Watkins referring to the pattern of energetic connection between ancient sacred sites such as Stonehenge and Salisbury Cathedral. Not restricted to England, ley lines are similar to energetic pathways within a world-wide mapping system which produce positive vortices of energy. Sedona, Arizona is said to be an example of ley lines and vortex power.

Life Aspirations the eight areas of living addressed as Life Areas within feng shui: Career, Wisdom & Knowledge, Family & Elders, Wealth & Abundance, Fame & Reputation, Love & Relationships, Children & Creativity, Helpful People & Travel. (see Appendices A and B).

luo pan (*pronounced lo pan*) the traditional feng shui compass used by practitioners containing concentric rings of Chinese words and symbols showing references required for Compass School analysis of a home, office, or building site.

Magic Square (Lo Shu)

the ancient mathematical construct of nine numbers arranged in three rows, so when added in any direction, total fifteen.

mirrors

used as a solution for numerous design challenges and to deflect sha chi.

mundane

having to do with a physical or simple feng shui application or cure, such as painting a dark-colored, heavy overhead beam white in order to make it visually disappear.

natal energy

the energetic qualities that are inherent in any property: location, direction, chi flow, Elements, Personal Directions, Flying Stars.

nine

considered a powerful number in feng shui, nine is the highest single digit. Often used in multiples, nine is used whenever possible, to enhance and empower a feng shui remedy.

Nourishing Cycle of the Elements

used constantly in feng shui to balance the design elements within a room or space: Fire produces ash (Earth), Earth generates Metal (ore), Metal holds Water, Water nourishes Wood, Wood feeds Fire.

pa kua

(pronounced pa kwa) Compass School spelling for bagua (see bagua), the energetic template used throughout feng shui practice. The eight trigrams of the *I Ching* arranged in the Later Heaven Sequence.

poison arrow

a design feature which has an intimidating influence over another, similar to a finger being pointed at you. Poison arrows in feng shui send negative energy toward a structure or interior space, and are to be avoided or mitigated whenever possible.

used in Black Sect School. Prior to any mystical feng shui solution being given from one person to another, the receiver gives the teacher a red envelope (or multiples of nine red envelopes) containing something of value. This tradition is considered extremely important, reflecting the pure intention of both giver and receiver of the solution. Following the Tradition of the Red Envelope demonstrates the respect of the student, honors the work performed, and protects the positive chi of the giver.

remedies interchangeable with "solutions" and "cures."

sha (chi) literally, "noxious vapor," the opposite of beneficial chi. Negative energy emanating from pointed corners, taller neighboring structures, power poles, nearby roof lines.

shui *(pronounced sch'way)* water or watercourse such as river, stream, or lake.

solutions feng shui remedies, a few examples are mirrors, wind chimes, or crystals. Solutions also involve the specific placement of these remedies.

tai chi *(pronounced tie chee)* the central area of the bagua depicted by the yin-yang symbol, which represents overall well-being and perfect balance of the environment under consideration. Considered to be the harmonious goal of feng shui design, and a power center within a specific space.

talismans Chinese mystical written blessings, often used on doorways, and when giving gifts. Used to ward off evil spirits, negative energy of all kinds, and to invoke the protective aspects of Heaven.

Taoism	*(pronounced Dowism),* a philosophy associated with Tao, "the Way," and is one of the original components of feng shui dating from ancient times. Actively practiced today, Taoism holds that beauty found in Nature is the ideal of perfection.
ti li	*(pronounced tee-lee)* name for feng shui in classical Chinese sources, translated as "land patterns" or in more modern times "geography" (Skinner, p. xi).
transcendental	referring to a more mystical aspect of feng shui.
trigrams	associated with the *I Ching,* or *Book of Changes,* the eight combinations of three solid or broken lines, one above the other, which represent various qualities or elements helpful to understanding the vicissitudes of life. By combining the trigrams in all their possible variations, the sixty-four hexagrams of the *I Ching* are produced.
wind chime	energy enhancer that employs movement and often sound. Used frequently in feng shui, both inside and outside to empower or raise the chi in a particular spot.
yang	heaven or male energy; associated with expansive spaces, brilliant light, heat, etc.
yi	the more transcendental or spiritual side of feng shui, the power of the spirit, will, and mind, concerned especially with the setting of intention to bring about specific desired results, used especially in BTB School.
yin	female or passive energy, associated with the receptive Element of Earth.

Bibliography

Alexander, Christopher. *A Pattern Language*. Oxford University Press. 1979.

------- *A Timeless Way of Building*. Oxford University Press. 1979.

Alexander, Jane. *Spirit of the Home*. Watson-Guptil Publications. 2000.

Bruss, Robert J. *The Robert Bruss Home Buyer's Workbook*. Tribune Publishing. 1991.

Collins, Terah Kathryn. *The Western Guide to Feng Shui*. Hay House. 1996.

Day, Christopher. *Places of the Soul*. Harper Collins. 1995.

Gadow, Sandy. *The Complete Guide to Your Real Estate Closing*. McGraw-Hill. 2002.

Glink, Ilyce R. *100 Questions Every First-Time Home Buyer Should Ask*. Three Rivers Press. 2002.

Hale, Gill. *The Practical Encyclopedia of Feng Shui*. Lorenz Books. 1999.

Irwin, Robert. *Tips and Traps When Buying a Home*. McGraw Hill. 1990.

------ *Pocket Guide for Home Buyers*. McGraw-Hill. 1998.

Kiplinger Editors. *Kiplinger's Buying and Selling a Home*. Kiplinger Books. 2002.

Lin, Jami. *The Essence of Feng Shui*. Hay House. 1998.
------- *Feng Shui Today*. Self published. 1997.
------- *Earth Design - The Added Dimension*. Earth Design, Inc. 1995.

Linn, Denise. *Feng Shui for the Soul*. Hay House. 1999
--------*Sacred Space*. Ballantine. 1995. Hay House. 1999.

Lo, Raymond. *Feng Shui Handbook*. Aquarian Press. 1991.

McLean, Andrew & Gary W. Eldred, Ph.D. *Investing in Real Estate*.
John Wiley & Sons. 2001.

Mann, A.T. *Sacred Architecture*. Element Publishers. 1993.

Molloy, William J. *The Complete Home Buyer's Bible*. John Wiley &
Sons. 1996.

Murray, Elizabeth. *Cultivating Sacred Space*. Pomegranate Publishers.
1995. 1997.

Pearson. *The Natural House Book*. Simon & Schuster/Fireside. 1989.
------- *The New Natural House Book*, Simon & Schuster/Fireside.
1998.

SantoPietro, Nancy. *Feng Shui: Harmony by Design*. Berkeley
Publishing Group. 1996.

Skinner, Stephen. *The Living Earth Manual of Feng Shui*.
Penguin-Arkana. 1989.
-------- *Feng Shui, the Traditional Chinese Way to Enhance your Life*.
Smithmark Publishers. 1998.
-------- *Flying Star Feng Shui*. Tuttle Publishing. 2003.

Spear, William. *Feng Shui Made Easy*. Harper. 1995.

Rossbach, Sarah and Lin Yun. *Living Color*. Kodansha International.
1994.

--------*Feng Shui Design*. Viking. 1998.

Rousseau, David & James Wasley. *Healthy by Design*. Hartley & Marx. 1997.

Stasney, Sharon. *Feng Shui Chic, Stylish Designs for Harmonious Living*. Sterling Publishers. 2000.

Tanzer, Elliot Jay. *Choose the Best House for You: the Feng Shui Checklist*. Elliot Jay Tanzer Publishing. 2003.

Too, Lillian. *The Fundamentals of Feng Shui*. Element Books. 1999.

Trevelyan, Joanna. *Holistic Home*. Sterling Publishing Co. 1998.

Venolia, Carol. *Healing Environments*. Celestial Arts Pub. 1988.

Walters, Derek. *The Feng Shui Handbook*. Thorsons Publishers. 1991.

Webster, Richard. *Feng Shui for Beginners*. Llewellyn Publications. 1997.

Meet Holly Ziegler, M.A., Ed.

Real Estate Broker • Feng Shui Consultant • Teacher
Author • Professional Speaker

Holly is a multimillion dollar producing real estate broker working from California's central coast since 1976. She has studied feng shui from highly recognized masters both in China and the United States for over a dozen years, and now teaches this ancient art of placement at the university level to other feng shui consultants, real estate professionals, and the general public.

She is the author of the best-selling books, *Sell Your Home FASTER with Feng Shui and Buy Your Home SMARTER with Feng Shui,* both of which are carried at the highest professional level by the National Association of REALTORS® and the California Association of

REALTORS®. Holly also coauthored the popular books *Feng Shui Your Work Space for Dummies* and *Feng Shui Your Garden for Dummies.*

Holly is a frequent guest on television and radio shows, is a much-requested speaker at conventions, and a speaker for public groups large and small. She contributes to national magazines and shares her expertise on feng shui and real estate through seminars for corporate clients, architectural firms, real estate companies, and advanced feng shui consultants.

Holly cofounded the *Feng Shui Association of the Central Coast* and writes feng shui columns for San Luis Obispo's *The Information Press.* She is producing several real estate/feng shui videos and audio cassettes.

Her much-in-demand feng shui consultations are geared to achieving dynamic results for residential and commercial clients. She travels nationally to teach classes and work one-on-one with REALTORS®, buyers, sellers, business owners, corporations, architects, and developers.

Helping others to design, buy, and sell their homes and achieving harmony, balance and overall well-being within their personal environment is her delight.

Holly Ziegler's Feng Shui Solutions
P.O. Box 1036 • Arroyo Grande, CA 93421

To schedule a consultation, receive class information, order autographed books, or for general inquiries, call Holly toll free:
1.888.869.2399

holly@fengshui-realestate.com ~ www.fengshui-realestate.com

Index

move in date, 19, 241

Easy Order Form

_____ copies of *Buy Your Home SMARTER with Feng Shui*
(Published at $19.95)

1-5	$19.95 ea. plus $ 8.95 shipping
6-11	$15.95 ea. plus $13.95 shipping
1 Dozen	$13.95 ea. plus $17.95 shipping
2 Dozen	$11.95 ea. plus $24.95 shipping
6 Dozen or more	$9.95 ea. and *free* shipping

_____ copies of *Sell Your Home FASTER with Feng Shui*
(Published at $16.95)

1-5	$16.95 ea. plus $ 8.95 shipping
6-11	$13.95 ea. plus $13.95 shipping
1 Dozen	$12.95 ea. plus $17.95 shipping
2 Dozen	$10.95 ea. plus $24.95 shipping
6 Dozen or more	$8.95 ea. and *free* shipping

Broker / Agent Discounts... Cheaper by the Dozen!

Mail to:

Holly Ziegler
P.O. Box 1036
Arroyo Grande, CA 93421

Telephone: (888) 869-2399
Fax (805) 489-4828
e-mail: Holly@FengShui-RealEstate.com

Subtotal	$ _____
Shipping	$ _____
Tax*	$ _____

*California residents, add 7.25% sales tax.

Total $ _____

Checks / MasterCard & Visa / Purchase Orders

Card #: _____ Circle one: MC Visa Expires: _____

Purchase Order #: _____ Signature: _____

Make checks payable to: Holly Ziegler

Ship to: _____

Address: _____

City: _____ State: _____ Zip: _____

Phone or e-mail:* _____

*if we have questions or need more information to promptly fill your order

<u>*Notes*</u>

Notes

Notes

<u>*Notes*</u>

Notes

Notes

Tear Out Section

Priority List for My New Home

Feng Shui Property Check List

As you preview property with your real estate professional, some homes will appeal to you more than others. When you get serious about a particular property, use this checklist to form a clear feng shui picture of how that house measures up energetically.

A significant number of negative items obviously indicates the house has poor feng shui. Do not let yourself be talked into purchasing unwisely. *These checklists can be removed from the book and you may photocopy them as often as necessary.* Good luck and have fun with this process!

Neighborhood

___ Are neighboring rooflines excessively pointy, sending sha chi your way? (-)

___ Is anything in front of, behind, or to the side of the house that is excessively tall, weighty, or massive? (-)

___ Are there large electric devices nearby? (-)

___ Are neighboring large satellite dishes or ham radio antennae aimed toward the house you are considering? (-)

___ Consider all neighboring influences, even those beyond your immediate street. Is there a nearby freeway being expanded, a new overpass built, or any busy street? How will the noise affect you? (-)

___ Is a zoning change bringing commercial or manufacturing into your neighborhood? (-) Ask your agent to investigate.

___ Will a school have bells and sports events with powerful lighting or loudspeakers? (-)

___ Are there churches, temples, synagogues, graveyards, hospitals, or mortuaries nearby? (-)

___ As you drive by after work hours, on weekends, and different times of the day (and evening), are there an excessive number of cars parked on streets? (-)

___ Overflow parking from the church around the corner? (-)

___ Unusual neighborhood noise? (-)

___ Is there a water tower, or large water storage tank nearby? (-)

___ Is the route to your prospective property unpleasant? (-)

___ Does the name of your potential street have a negative energetic association for you? (-)

___ If on a cul-de-sac, is it at the top of the closed street? (- -)

Parcel of Land

___ Does the property have some energetically supporting feature at the rear, such as a hill, healthy trees, substantial rocks, tall shrubs, a solid wall or fence? (+)

___ Does the parcel have some sort of protective foliage or sturdy fencing on both sides of the house? (+)

___ Does the land slope down from the house in the rear? (-)

___ Is there a pleasant view to the front of the property? (+)

___ It takes a long time to grow a majestic tree. Property with mature landscaping gets extra points. (+)

___ Is the lot on or close to the top of a hill? (-)

___ Located on a T or Y intersection? (- -) If so, keep looking.

___ Is the house situated on an outside curve? (-)

___ Is it on an inside curve? (+)

House Exterior

___ Are the porch and front door visible from the street? (+)

___ Does the front path curve gently? (+) or is it straight and rigid? (-)

___ Does the house address contain or add up to your lucky number? (+)

___ Are the house numbers easily seen from the street? (+)

___ Is the porch slightly elevated? (+)

___ Is there room for a fountain near the front door? (+)

___ Is the porch sheltered by a roof or arbor? (+)

___ Does your front door look across to a neighbor's driveway or garage? (-)

___ Is the main door strong, solid, and in good condition? (+)

___ Does the main door need replacing or repainting? (-)

___ If there is a screen door, is it rusty, bent, or dented? (-)

___ Is the threshold solid when stepped on? (+)

___ Is the doorknob solid and firm to the grip? (+)

___ Does the key fit into the door without difficulty? (+)

House Interior

___ As you view the interior of a house, think carefully about how the sun affects each room. How many lights will you need during the day to live comfortably? Many? (-) Few or none (+)

___ Are there "arguing," "biting," or "contrary" doors? (-)

___ Is the front door in line with the back door or sliding doors? (-)

___ Are the windows in proportion to the doors? (+)

___ Do all windows open and are the locks in good condition? (+)

___ Does the house have a spiral staircase? (-)

___ Do any stairways have open risers? (-)

___ Are there interior beams or structural roof supports? (-)

___ Any interior posts or pillars? (-)

___ Sloping ceilings over sitting or sleeping areas? (-)

___ Is there a long, poorly lit hallway? (-)

___ Does the house have seriously negative "precursor" energy? (- -)

Entry/Foyer

___ Is the entry open and light (+) or small and dark? (-)

___ Can you add a skylight if necessary? (+)

___ Is there a staircase in front of the main door? (- -)

___ Can you see the kitchen or a bathroom from the entry? (-)

___ Is the size of the entry adequate for chi to circulate easily before entering the rest of the house? (+)

Master Bedroom

___ Located in the right rear (or southwest) corner of the house? (+)

___ Located behind the house mid-line? (+)

___ Allow for bed placement in a command position? (+)

___ Does the bed placement allow you to sleep with your head pointing toward one of your Positive Directions? (See Special Supplement.) (+)

___ Is the bed on the other side of a wall from a bathroom or toilet? (-)

___ Is there a closeable door separating the bedroom from the bathroom? (+)

Kitchen

___ Located in front of the house mid-line? (+)

___ Will you face the main kitchen door when cooking? (+)

___ Does a bathroom or toilet share a wall with the kitchen? (-)

___ Is a bathroom located above the kitchen? (-)

___ Is the toilet on the floor overhead above the stove? (-)

Office

___ Is there room for good chi circulation around your desk? (+)

___ Will your desk and chair command the door? (+)

___ Will your chair face one of your Best Directions? (+)

___ Will there be a window behind your desk (-) or a solid wall? (+)

___ Does your potential office have plenty of natural sunlight? (+)

Dining Room

___ If entertaining is important, will the location of the table put you in the command position and still away from the kitchen door? (+)

___ Will the table placement allow you face one of your Best Directions? (+)

___ Is the room naturally lit with good circulating chi around the table? (+)

Living Room / Great Room

___ Naturally light and spacious? (+)

___ Is there a window with a good view? (+)

___ Room for chi to circulate for various activities? (+)

___ Located in front of the mid-line of the house? (+)

Family Room

___ Adjacent to kitchen and eating area? (+)

___ Adequate space to accommodate family activities? (+)

___ In front of the mid-line of the house? (+)

Bathrooms / Laundry Room

___ Is a bathroom or laundry located in the center or tai chi area? (- -) If so, go on to the next house.

___ Is a bathroom in the Wealth (SE) or Romance (SW) area? (-)

___ Does a bathroom or toilet share a wall with the kitchen? (-)

Garage

___ Adjacent to a yin function room such as the master bedroom? (-)

___ If a two level home, is the garage under the master or any other bedroom? (-)

Totals   (+) _____   (-) _____

Feng Shui Deal Breakers

Despite a positive outlook and valiant feng shui attempts to make a "silk purse out of a sow's ear," there are a few aspects of a property that defy good energetic results. These are considered feng shui "deal breakers" and *properties with these chi challenges should be avoided.*

- ☯ Floor plan with a bathroom located in the central tai chi area
- ☯ Property located at a heavily trafficked T or a Y junction road
- ☯ Excessively odd-shaped house with serious missing Life Aspirations, especially Wealth, Romance, or Career
- ☯ Structure built over an ancient burial ground, cemetery, or slaughterhouse
- ☯ Dwelling or office with seriously negative pre-cursor energy
- ☯ Structure built at the edge of a cliff or precipice
- ☯ Property situated at the bottom of a ravine or canyon
- ☯ House near excessive noise or obnoxious odors
- ☯ Property located close to a major electric transformer, large power lines, microwave cell phone transmitter, or power generator
- ☯ Structure built over reclaimed wetlands or hazardous waste disposal site
- ☯ Property with a swiftly flowing water feature behind
- ☯ Floor plan with a spiral staircase in the center
- ☯ Floor plan with a staircase directly in front of the main door

Feng Shui Property Appraisal™

My feelings score: ☐

Property Address: _____

Listing Office: _____

Shown to me by: (agent or owner) _____

Date of showing: _____ Approx. time of day: _____

Drawing of floor plan:

Front door compass reading (N, SW, E, etc.) ____ Degrees: _____

My 4 Positive Personal Directions are: _____

When sleeping, my bed will command the door: (Yes or No)

The direction my head will point when sleeping: _____

When cooking, I will command the door: (Yes or No)

The direction I will face when cooking: _____

Seated at my desk, I will command the door: (Yes or No)

The direction I will face when seated at my desk: _____